HOCKEY HALL OF FAME TREASURES

HOCKEY
HALL *of* FAME
TREASURES

Foreword *by* Scotty Bowman | Photographs *by* Matthew Manor

Edited *by* Steve Cameron

 HOCKEY HALL *of* FAME

FIREFLY BOOKS

A FIREFLY BOOK

Published by Firefly Books Ltd. 2011
Copyright © 2011 Firefly Books Ltd.
Text copyright © 2011 Hockey Hall of Fame
Images copyright as listed on page 205.
All rights reserved.

First printing

Published in the United States by
Firefly Books (U.S.) Inc.
P.O. Box 1338, Ellicott Station
Buffalo, New York 14205

Published in Canada by
Firefly Books Ltd.
66 Leek Crescent
Richmond Hill, Ontario L4B 1H1

Copyedit and index: Nancy Foran
Cover and interior design: Counterpunch Inc. / Peter Ross

Printed in China

The publisher gratefully acknowledges the financial support for our publishing program by the Government of Canada through the Canada Book Fund as administered by the Department of Canadian Heritage.

Publisher Cataloging-in-Publication Data (U.S.)
Cameron, Steve, 1981-
   Hockey Hall of Fame treasures / edited by Steve Cameron ; foreword by Scotty Bowman ; photographs by Matthew Manor. [224] p. : photos. ; cm. Includes index.
Summary: A showcase of the most interesting, unique, famous and exciting artifacts from the Hockey Hall of Fame's collection, with essays on hockey by Dave Bidini, Adrienne Clarkson, James Duthie and Don Gillmor.

ISBN-13: 978-1-55407-887-5
1. Hockey Hall of Fame. 2. National Hockey League –Miscellanea. 3. Hockey players – Pictorial works I. Bowman, Scotty. II. Manor, Matthew. III. Title.
796.962/27   dc22   GV848.76C3647   2011

Library and Archives Canada Cataloguing in Publication
   Hockey Hall of Fame treasures / edited by Steve Cameron ; foreword by Scotty Bowman; photographs by Matthew Manor. Includes index.

ISBN 978-1-55407-887-5
1. Hockey Hall of Fame – Miscellanea. 2. Hockey – Miscellanea. 3. Hockey – History. I. Cameron, Steve, 1981-
GV847.H555 2011   796.962   C2011-904222-3

PAGE 2: Face-molded goalie masks. *Top row, from left to right:* Jim Rutherford's Detroit Red Wings mask from the 1974–75 season; this mask was the first to ever be painted with a design, heralding a tradition that is now a calling card of the game. New York Islanders mask worn by Glenn "Chico" Resch from 1974 to 1976. John Garrett's Hartford Whalers mask, worn during the 1980–81 and 1981–82 NHL seasons. *Bottom row, from left to right:* Edmonton Oilers mask worn by Grant Fuhr during the 1983–84 and 1984–85 NHL seasons. Kim Crouch, who famously suffered a neck laceration in 1975 that led to the creation of the neck guard (also known as the Kim Crouch Collar), wore this mask while playing Junior B for the Markham Waxers in 1975–76. Gilles Meloche's Cleveland Barons mask, worn during 1977–78 NHL season.

Gold medal won by Great Britain's Gerry Davey at the 1936 Winter Olympics, held in Garmisch-Partenkirchen, Germany. Davey led the British team in goals, with seven, as Britain became the first non-Canadian team to win Olympic hockey gold.

CONTENTS

Foreword: Scotty Bowman   8

Introduction: Philip Pritchard   10

1   **Celebrating the Game**   12
    Moments to Mementos by Dave Bidini   21

2   **Playing the Game**   38
    The Prodigal Son by Don Gillmor   73
    Highways of Hockey by Dave Bidini   111

3   **Honoring the Game**   148
    The Birth of the Clarkson Cup by Adrienne Clarkson   161

4   **Recording the Game**   176
    Reporting the Game by James Duthie   185

    Afterword: Preserving Hockey History at
    the Hockey Hall of Fame by Risto Pakarinen   198

    Acknowledgments   205

    Extended Captions   206

    Index   222

The original Stanley Cup bowl, professionally engraved with the names of championship teams and amateurishly scrawled with the scratchings of championship-team members, including Fred W. Taylor (also known as "Cyclone"). Taylor won the Cup with Ottawa in 1909 and with Vancouver in 1915. He was highly regarded in his day and is now considered by many to be the best hockey player of his era.

FOREWORD

| **SCOTTY BOWMAN**

The Hockey Hall of Fame contains innumerable treasures, and many of the best and most famous of them are found in this book. And while it may be cliché to call the Hockey Hall of Fame a shrine, that's exactly what it is – a shrine for all of hockey.

Hockey is such a beautiful, deep and quickly evolving game that I can't imagine how we could ever keep track of it, or fully appreciate its scope, without the Hockey Hall of Fame. People often think only about the NHL when they visit the Hall, but there's more depth to the collection than most realize. The amount of interesting and educational items from other leagues and other levels of hockey in Canada, the United States and throughout the world help illustrate how many different people are deeply involved in hockey and how much the game is a part of people's lives, not only in North America but all over the world. I think it's very important to expose people to the history of the game. If we can understand where hockey comes from and see how its equipment, uniforms, style of play, reporting and broadcasting have evolved, we can develop a much better feel for today's game and a better understanding of where hockey might go in the future.

When people start following hockey, one of the things they find most difficult to grasp is that there was a time when goalies didn't wear masks. I was working for the Canadiens when Jacques Plante got hurt during a game in New York and came back out wearing a mask after getting stitched up. That mask would be the first one regularly worn in NHL action. The big question surrounding masks at the time wasn't goalie safety but whether a

goalie's vision would be negatively impacted, especially when looking down at his feet. The Hockey Hall of Fame has done a great job showcasing some of the most memorable masks, as well as the evolution of those masks.

Advancements in equipment have always been fascinating to me. Early helmets were made completely of leather, so you wonder what kind of protection they could have provided. It's the same with so many other pieces of equipment that are on display in the Hall. Take, for example, the size of the equipment. The old goalie pads rose just barely above a goalie's knees. They were all handmade by Emil "Pop" Kenesky, and you had to get in line to get a pair – you couldn't just pick them up off a store shelf. Those old pads would soak up water too, which made them heavier as a game went on, same as the wool sweaters players used to wear.

The old hockey sticks are among my favorite artifacts in the Hall of Fame, especially the first curved sticks used by Stan Mikita and Bobby Hull. It amazes me that something now considered so fundamental to the game was discovered by accident. Another part of the Hall of Fame that I thoroughly enjoy is the recreation of the Montreal Canadiens' dressing room. I spent a lot of time in that dressing room at the Forum over the eight years I was with the Canadiens. It was always a special place to me. The thing that sets it apart from other NHL dressing rooms is the quote, painted on the wall, from John McCrae's poem "In Flanders Field": "To you from failing hands we throw the torch."

I appreciate the collection even more because I'm a collector of hockey memorabilia myself. My collecting didn't start until the early 1980s, when my two boys became interested in hockey cards. We collected old cards and new cards and hunted for the cards of popular players. My brother lived near a card manufacturer, and he would get us whole uncut sheets of the new card sets, which are fairly rare. Then I branched out into collecting other hockey items. I've got four letters from American presidents, one for each of the four times I went to the White House after winning the Stanley Cup with American-based teams. I also have a letter from Pierre Elliot Trudeau congratulating me on a Team Canada win. I've got two seats from the Montreal Forum, which the team gave to me when they decommissioned that venerable building. And at the end of each hockey season I get a stick signed by the players and coaches of every team I'm with. I've also got a lot of hockey items from Russia, including a pair of gloves that were given to me by Anatoly Tarasov, the architect of Russian hockey.

Treasures of the Hockey Hall of Fame helps us grasp the incredible reach and history of our favorite game. When I first started working for Montreal, with the Ottawa Junior Canadiens in 1956, I became friends with Dr. Sandy Watson, who was the team physician for the Royal Canadian Air Force Flyers hockey club – Canada's entry at the 1948 Winter Olympics. George Mara, who sat on the board of the Toronto Maple Leafs, was also a member of that team. When I saw an RCAF Flyers exhibit at the Hall it was like seeing their stories come to life.

Elite amateur hockey of the 20th century, especially in Canada, provided tremendous and exciting action that sometimes rivaled that of NHL hockey. It used to be that the winner of the Allan Cup, awarded to the best amateur team in Canada, would represent Canada internationally at the Olympics and at World Championships. There was a lot of good, important hockey played by these teams, as well as the amateur junior teams that competed nationally for the Memorial Cup. The smaller communities in Canada and the United States that support these teams may love the NHL, but their hearts are with the hometown teams. That's why I love to see the displays at the Hall representing the Allan Cup and Memorial Cup teams and the teams they played against on the way to winning. I feel it is here that you can most closely see the link between hockey and everyday life.

There are so many treasures and little gems in the Hall of Fame that it's hard to get a sense of the breadth of the collection without actually going there. The experience of being at the Hockey Hall of Fame is enhanced not only by the majesty of the Honored Members section and the historical importance of the thousands of artifacts, but also by the people connected to and working for the Hockey Hall of Fame. For them, preserving and celebrating hockey history is not a job; it is a way of life – just like hockey itself. Enjoy this book. It is the next best thing to being at the Hockey Hall of Fame.

SCOTTY BOWMAN is the NHL's winningest coach, with 1,244 victories, and has captured more Stanley Cups than any other bench boss, with nine. He was inducted into the Hockey Hall of Fame in the builder category in 1991.

INTRODUCTION

| **PHILIP PRITCHARD**

Turning the pages of *Hockey Hall of Fame Treasures*, I am reminded of why I got interested in hockey and collecting in the first place.

Like many Canadian kids, when I was growing up, hockey was a pretty big part of my life. I collected hockey cards, played road hockey and idolized the stars of the NHL. The Habs were my team and Rogie Vachon my guy, even though Montreal had traded him to Los Angeles. My parents, on the other hand, were British, and they didn't get it.

I don't know when my hockey obsession started, but I clearly remember when I started collecting. I was walking by Buddy Fugard's house on my way home from school when I was 11 years old, and Buddy had his garbage out at the curb. Resting on top of a pile of magazines was a 1969 *Maple Leaf Gardens Hockey Magazine*. I very quickly made the decision to bring it home with me.

My collecting really took off two years later. I can't remember what I had done, but my parents grounded me for an entire week. If you were to ask my mom she'd say that I was grounded so often that she can't remember one grounding from the next. But this weeklong grounding is something I remember vividly because the punishment couldn't possibly have fit the crime: my parents grounded me from the one thing that I really cared about, hockey! And it wasn't just playing, I couldn't watch, read or listen to the game either.

It was late March and the playoffs were in full swing. Now, I am sure the NHL playoffs were in full swing as well, but the playoffs I'm talking about were our road hockey playoffs. My entire childhood seemed like a big hockey game, as every day and no matter the season, after school, after dinner, weekends and summer holidays we were always playing road hockey. We had a great street to play on, a dead end with only 10 houses, which minimized the interruptions. Most of our neighbors knew we played daily and would drive around our nets so that we didn't have to move them. We even kept stats, and any kid could have told you that the Birdcage Bombers were the team to beat!

The first night of my grounding, I came home from school and had to immediately start my homework. It was Monday night, and from my window I could hear the game on the street. I instantly flew to my window, took out the screen and for a moment I became Foster Hewitt as I called the game from my bedroom. Of course, my play-by-play lasted only as long as my dad was at work, and before long I was back at my homework.

As the week progressed, my play-by-play became better, but to pass the rest of the time I was grounded I began to clean and decorate my room. I may have been grounded from hockey, but what was there to stop me from turning my room into a hockey shrine? The walls, the shelves, even the ceiling all slowly became consumed by "Phil's hockey shrine." Cards, pennants, magazines, books, mugs, stamps, coins, posters, whatever had hockey on it was something I wanted for my room. I even banned my mom from dusting – she could have broken something! What kind of teenager says that to his mom?

When the weeklong grounding was over the flood gates opened. All the autographs I had written away for during the grounding started to come in, as did the stuff I got from sending in my box tops, and I also bought all the posters I had saved up for.

Somewhere along the way I folded under peer pressure and allowed girls into my life. And wouldn't you know it, it was 1979–80, the same season that Wayne Gretzky joined the NHL and his card was the one to get. Except I didn't collect hockey cards that year because, apparently, girls were better.

Thankfully I got my head screwed back on right and collecting again became my passion. The Locker Room, the ultimate collectors store, got all of my allowance and eventually all of my earnings from my two summer jobs, a pinsetter at the local bowling alley and an attendant at the gas station.

Now I look back fondly over the years that have passed and think about how lucky I am. All those years of clipping, trading, collecting and sending away, and I am now fortunate enough to be the curator of the Hockey Hall of Fame. Even my parents get it now.

Of course, my job isn't a solo act, nor is it something that I started. The Hockey Hall of Fame wouldn't exist without the vision of Clarence Campbell and the owners of the Original Six teams that addressed the need for a hockey shrine. Without Bobby Hewitson and Maurice H. "Lefty" Reid, the archival collection wouldn't exist. And without the diligent work of Ralph Dinger, Ray Paquet, Barry Eversley, Joseph Romain, James Duplacey, Jeff Davis, Esther Richards, Jane Rodney, Karyn Lisa Knott and Danielle Siciliano, to name just a few, as well as today's fabulous staff, the Hockey Hall of Fame would not be the world's marquee sports museum and hall of fame.

Hockey Hall of Fame Treasures is the celebration of the combined efforts of all of these people, as well as the generous donations from players, managers, teams, leagues, families and fans who have thought enough of the Hockey Hall of Fame over the years to extend us the pleasure of preserving and displaying their prized hockey possessions.

Former president Ian "Scotty" Morrison once called the Hockey Hall of Fame "the cathedral of the icons of hockey." We now have it in book form, and I hope you enjoy viewing our collection as much as all of us here have enjoyed collecting it.

Game on!

PHILIP PRITCHARD, lifelong hockey fan and vice president and curator of the Hockey Hall of Fame.

CELEBRATING

THE GAME

The ultimate way to celebrate the game is to be there at rink side. However, the physical act of cheering is fleeting and only a small part of celebrating the game. Long after the final whistle blows and the arena is empty, it is the shared memories and the celebration that happens in the day-to-day lives of fans that keep fandom strong between games and across generations.

The tangible keepsakes, collectibles, swag and personal mementos are ways in which fans define themselves and their relationship with the game. Wearing the logo of a particular league, team or player enables a fan to find a community of like-minded people, all rooting for the same thing. To collect or exhibit items that illustrate your favorite team or player is a definitive sign of fandom. From hockey cards and action figures to pinball games and replica jerseys, the message comes across loud and clear: "I am a hockey fan."

As Dave Bidini says in his essay "Moments to Mementos," "[these items] recount the richness of experience that is often too long or tiresome to express to ourselves and to others. Instead, the hockey fan can point to a puck or a stick or a pin, and, in the lingua franca of sports, others suddenly understand…. They're part of an inexpressible shorthand."

Presented in the following pages are items and moments belonging to that shorthand – objects of expression and desire, used and discarded by some and cherished by others – all of which contribute to our communal celebration of the game.

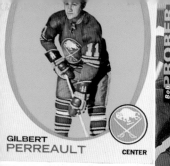

GILBERT
PERREAULT

CENTER

PROBER

CLARENCE DAY

WORLD JUNIOR CHAMPIONS

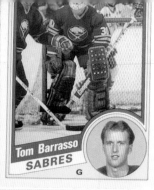

Tom Barrasso
SABRES

G

DANIEL ALFRE

OTTAWA SENATORS • RIGHT WING • AIL

MAPLE LEAFS

RON ELLIS

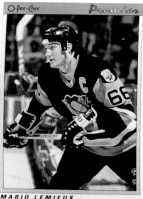

Alexander Mogilny

Left Wing

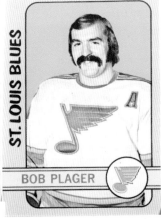

O-Pee-Chee

Premier

MARIO LEMIEUX
PENGUINS • CENTER/CENTRE

ST. LOUIS BLUES

BOB PLAGER

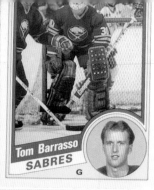

NEW YORK
RANGERS

Lorne Worsley Goalie

Ray Bourque
BRUINS

D

Terry
Sawchuk

John Slaney

Defense

WORLD JUNIOR CHAMPIONS

N92

PERCY LESUEUR of Ottawa Club

PRO
SET

1973-74 NHL EA
ALL-STAR

Mike Modano

B

BRU

BOBB

ULF NILSSON
JETS C

46
GOAL

Johnny Bowers

O-Pee-Chee

MARK MESSIER
EDMONTON OILERS

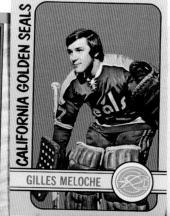

CALIFORNIA GOLDEN SEALS

GILLES MELOCHE

S. MANTHA

NORTH STARS

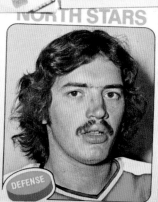

DEFENSE

IT BIALOWAS

Premier

A
16

NORTH STARS

toronto MAPLE LEAFS

SCORE

A PINNACLE BRAND

TORONTO
MAPLE
LEAFS

Ron Stewart

RIGHT
WING

B

PARKHURST

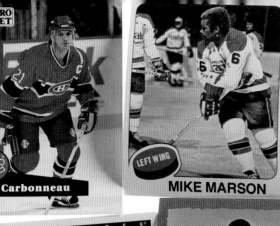

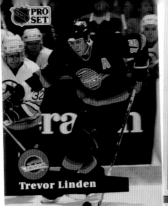

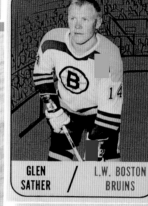

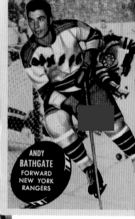

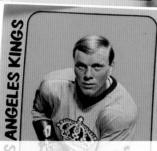

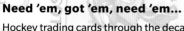

Need 'em, got 'em, need 'em...

Hockey trading cards through the decades. The cards here range from the earliest tobacco and bubble gum cards, featuring illustrations and colored black-and-white photography, to the sleek laminated, die-cut and full-color cards of today.

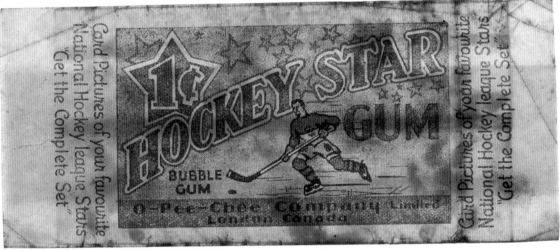

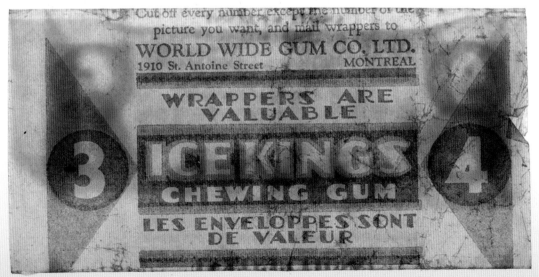

◄ Wax gum wrappers from the early days of the NHL. Gum companies, such as World Wide Gum from Montreal, Quebec, and Hamilton Chewing Gum from Hamilton, Ontario, packaged hockey cards with their gum to boost sales. Consumers would purchase the gum with the hope of collecting the complete set of hockey cards, as pitched on the O-Pee-Chee Hockey Star Gum package seen here.

► An album from the early 1900s that was used to collect cigarette cards. Unless being trading among friends, there was no aftermarket value for hockey cards – unlike today. As such, cards were often pasted directly to the pages of albums such as this one.

Bill Cook

Cigarette
Cards

Gordie Howe in competition during the 1970–71 season. On the right is the famous "American flag" Gordie Howe hockey card from the 1963–64 Parkhurst set – Parkhurst's last – which featured Toronto, Montreal and Detroit. All Red Wings players were fitted with an American flag backdrop, and the Maple Leafs were anchored by the flag of the Dominion of Canada (as Canada did not yet have its own national flag). The Canadiens were flagless, pictured instead against multiple colored bars.

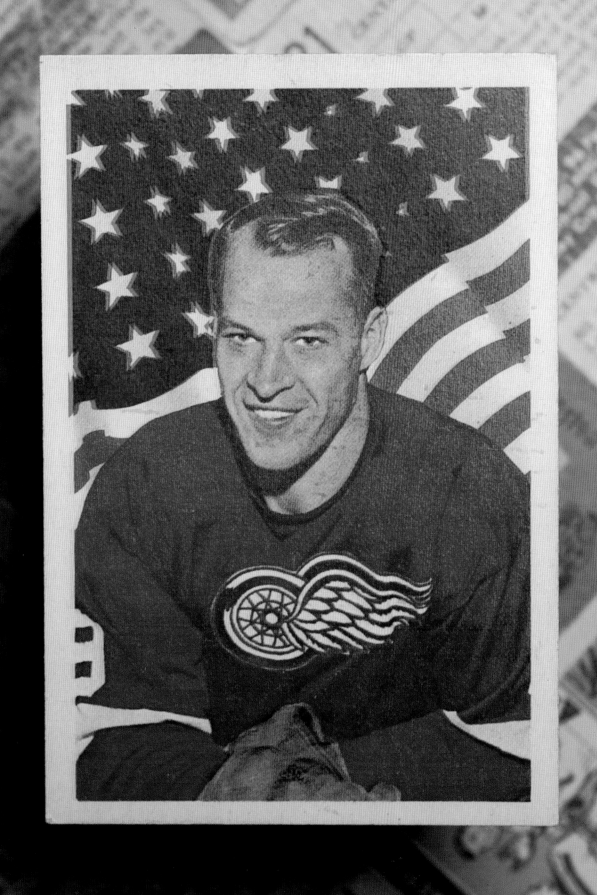

Arena of Dreams

Pieces from the Hockey Hall of Fame's collection of figurines and action figures in action. Joe Sakic looks to pass through the coverage of Cam Neely to Wayne Gretzky, who is being hounded by none other than "Rocket" Richard.

MOMENTS TO MEMENTOS

| **DAVE BIDINI**

Away from the rink, my hockey life is measured out in memorabilia: crests, decals, pins, cards, pennants, programs, buttons, iron-ons, stickers, books, postcards, scarves, records, sticks and one small, ancient equipment bag from the 1961 Toronto Maple Leafs, which was passed over a crowd to me while I was performing at Toronto's Horseshoe Tavern. I also have a life-sized Wendel Clark cutout. It was stolen from a sporting goods store, but not by me. The thief's name is Gary. He is a drummer from Calgary who is legally blind. Still, he can sniff out prized memorabilia as good as anyone. During the Leafs' playoff run in 1993, Gary brought the Wendel cutout to a show my band was playing at the El Mocambo in Toronto. I left with it under my arm; me and my cardboard Wendel, navigating our way through a spring night.

Hockey is about games and players, but it's also about this kind of stuff. I have a mountain of it here, there and in my basement, and so do you. And so does the Hockey Hall of Fame. But the Hall of Fame doesn't have what you and I have. While our things may not hold as much historical importance as the items displayed at the Hall, or be decorated with Bugsy Watson's blood, they do possess a certain magical weight – something that can only be achieved through profound personal connection. And that connection becomes important when we call upon our stuff as a way to remember our lives or define who we are – especially when explaining our relationship with hockey to someone who doesn't quite get it.

There's a chestnut sitting in an antique ashtray on top of the wardrobe in my bedroom. Technically it's a hawthorn berry, but it looks like a chestnut, only a little smaller. I was given this chestnut by a vendor in Harbin, China's ancestral homeland of hockey. I'd just finished playing there for two weeks with a team of ex-pat Americans from Pea Pack, New Jersey. We played games against Chinese old-timers as well as teenagers who represented the next generation of Harbinian hockey players. On our way to the train station we passed a nut vendor. I was dragging my hockey bag and stick – and luggage, ugh – with me, and this apparel amused the vendor to no end. He came out from behind his cart and grabbed my stick. Fearing that I would be late for our train, I tried to wrest it away from him, but he resisted, so I reached for his tray of nuts as a way to divert his attention. He put down my stick, laughed, went over, grabbed one of the nuts and fitted it between his teeth. He made a guttural "Nrrrgghggg!" sound as he bit down and smiled. Standing in the cold of northern China with this strange, grunting man is one of my most vivid memories of that trip. He spat the nut back into his hand, and I held out my palm. He laughed, nodded his head, then gave it to me. My kids call it my lucky chestnut. I suppose it is.

I had an altogether different, but similar, experience in Russia. It was 2005, and I was expected for an 11 p.m. game at a local rink about 40 minutes outside of Moscow. The team, I was told, consisted of veterans of the Soviet Union's Afghanistan war, though none of the organizers could substantiate this. I'd spent most of that afternoon at the apartment of 1972 Team Russia veteran Yuri Blinov. Yuri has cats – lots of cats – and, since I am allergic to them, I left our interview barely able to gasp for air. Sucking on my inhaler as we made our way to the rink in the late evening, I wondered whether I'd have the energy – the air – to skate that night. The people with whom I was traveling convinced me to go anyway. When I showed up at the rink, I could barely muster the strength to put on my equipment. I was an embarrassment on the ice. At one point, a player asked me, in broken English, "Have you played since you were a boy?" I told him that I had. "Then why are you so bad?" he wanted to know.

I had no good answer. After the game, we tore off our equipment, at which point I noticed the players' chests: scraped and carved and decorated in crude Russian tattoos, all of them worn while fighting in the Afghani mountains in the 1980s. Settling in front of our stalls, the players told us war stories and illuminated us about what Russian life had been like before and after the fall of Communism. Then the team's ringleader – a former soldier turned convict turned free citizen named Misha – made a phone call, and, 10 minutes later, a boy appeared carrying 12 Heineken tall boys and a bag of *deetchka*, Russian dope.

We drank and talked deep into the night, and, before leaving, a player whose name I was never told gave me a gift: an Orthodox Russian prayer cloth that, he said, his mother had given to him before he had headed to war. I told him that I couldn't possibly have it, but he insisted, pressing it into my hand with his. "It gave me very good luck," he told me. "And now, it will give you good luck."

But why would a soldier give away his lucky charm? I wanted to know. He told me that he was already lucky: he had survived the war and was back playing the game he loved best. The prayer cloth – dark purple with gold and silver Cyrillic lettering across it – now sits in a drawer just below my lucky chestnut.

There are other items that keep my Sino-Russian collection company: Mongolian sheep bones that two Asian hockey elders gave to me before I left Ulan Baatar and a specially made sweater from Al Ain, the desert town in the United Arab Emirates where the national team makes its home. One item I didn't bring home but wanted to is two pounds of smoked bacon, brought to me after a night of showing hockey films in an old Transylvanian town. Instead, we left it for our hotel clerk. In Romania, it's actually what I left behind that counted more than what I brought home with me. There, a local hockey manager planted a wild cherry tree for my newborn daughter. Today, it's 11 years old, 6 feet tall and blossoms every spring.

All of these things – my chestnut, my prayer cloth, the bones, the bacon and the cherry tree – reveal something about my life – where I've been, who I was, what I was doing – when I found them and when they found me. That they've stayed with me while other memories (and tokens) of people and places have become lost, in reality and in the recesses of my memory, shows how connected the game is to my sense of self and to my sense of time.

I've collected a lot of things as an adult, but never as much as I collected as a kid.

I've kept many of my childhood hockey mementos. Flipping through my weathered *Esso Power Player* album with Paul Henderson's looping signature on the back page is to return to the days of lying on my stomach in front of the wood-grained Zenith television that sat in our wood-grained basement. Of course, I have hockey cards, too, wound in old rubber bands and stacked team-to-team and year-to-year on a shelf in my office. There is the WHA fold-out mini-posters that were included in some Cream of Wheat or Rice Krispies boxes (only Mike Walton of the New England Fighting Saints remains) and flats of 80s puffy stickers with relief headshots documenting the first wave of Europeanalia: Nilson, Salming, Lidstrom, Bubla, et al.

I still even have a set of Gary Unger–era St. Louis Blues postcards, which I've resisted mailing, even though I have scads of friends who'd be delirious to find one of them dropping through

---

Hockey Night at the Kitchen Table

Many a fan has celebrated the game by playing table hockey. Shown here are games ranging from the 1950s and the Original Six era to modern boards featuring current NHL teams.

their mail slot. I've kept programs and boxes of old *Hockey Pictorial* magazines, which evoke the scent of old smoke shops, bubblegum and cigars, and what it felt like to stand, as a boy, in the glow of the shop's warm light with my father, who would reach into his pocket to jangle the dollar fifty required to purchase what, back then, was one of the game's true pictorial bibles.

I have photos, too. My most treasured is a set of crudely snapped Instamatic images I took of Team Canada 74 and their game against the Russians at Maple Leaf Gardens in Toronto. In one series, you can't see much more than the rows of larger adults sitting in front of me and, down below, on the ice, the back of Bobby Hull's head, whose thinning hair (or hair piece, perhaps?) couldn't quite hide his bald patch. With the photo comes the memory of Gardens' popcorn, the rattling of the clapped-up seats, the shrill cry of the organ, the grumbling of the crowd whenever the team fell behind, the sudden expression of joy after a goal or great play, and the heat of the arena in the early fall, which closed in on us as we took our seats for the big game.

In the end, a lot of these tokens are just that, ephemera that lingers on shelves, in the basement, in drawers, atop old furniture. But they're here for a reason: they recount the richness of experience that is often too long or tiresome to express to ourselves and to others. Instead, the hockey fan can point to a puck or a stick or a pin, and, in the lingua franca of sports, others suddenly understand. Sometimes expressing one's love and devotion to hockey will fall on deaf ears. But anyone can hold a magic chestnut or bits of a broken blade in their hands and understand. They're part of an inexpressible shorthand, and, although grounded and flightless, they still seem somehow alive to us – and to others.

Among all the things I have kept over the years, I still have a Toronto Toros crest. It is huge, the kind you put on the back of a jean jacket. I can't remember where I got it, but I do remember that the Toros were *it* in my neighborhood in 1974, the one year they rivaled the Leafs in popularity.

A few weeks ago, a friend of mine, also bitten by the Toros bug, who'd relocated to New York, gotten married and started a family was delivered a set of boxes from his mother. She'd taken to cleaning out the family basement and decided to return his childhood keepsakes. My friend told me how thrilled he was to have some of his boyhood tokens on hand, and how he planned to pass them on to his son. He said, excitedly, "You'll never, ever guess what she brought me!" But I didn't have to guess. I knew exactly what it was.

DAVE BIDINI, the Hockey Nomad, is a musician, journalist and author. He was a founding member of the acclaimed rock band the Rheostatics and has written several books, including *Tropic of Hockey* and *Home and Away: In Search of Dreams at the Homeless World Cup of Soccer*.

Manufacturing Mementos
Punch Imlach and the boys take a moment to autograph souvenir sticks in Toronto in the 1960s.

Canadien

CLEVELAND BARONS

CCCP
USA
RUSSIA
CANADA
SWEDEN
WEST GERMANY
CZECHOSLOVAKIA

TEAM CANADA

SCOUTS

BLACKHAWKS

Opening Night –
November 2, 1974

3
Score

4
Score

VS.

NHL

MOSCOW IZVESTIA

NHL FUTURE STARS '78

Vancouver Canucks

"CHUCK CANUCK"

MÜNCHEN

EISHOCKEY MÜNCHEN

Pennants celebrating various teams, leagues and eras from

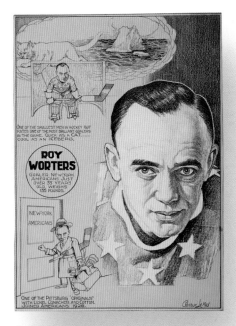

Arthur LeMay (Canadian, 1900–1944)

Roy Worters, 1935

Ink on paper

9.75 x 13.75 in. (25 x 35 cm)

Thompson (Unknown)

Hockey Hall of Fame Opening Ceremony, circa 1975

Acrylic on canvas

31.5 x 20.5 in. (80 x 52 cm)

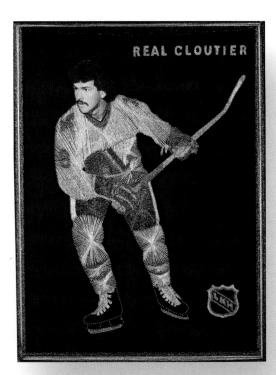

Artist Unknown

Real Cloutier, circa 1983

Metallic thread, nail and canvas on wooden board

28 x 37 in. (71 x 94 cm)

Dennis Maggs (Canadian, unknown)

Jean Béliveau, 1972

Oil on canvas

72 x 54 in. (183 x 137 cm)

Andy Warhol (American, 1928–1987), *Rod Gilbert, Athlete Series,* 1977–79
Silkscreen and polymer paint on canvas, 40 x 40 in. (102 x 102 cm)

Fan Appreciation

Bryan Trottier pumps his fist in the air in celebration. The cheer, shared with the fans around him, was directed toward Pat and Warren Amendola (off camera), the couple he boarded with on Long Island during his rookie season of 1975–76. To the left, Bobby Hull's head is seen poking out of a mob of children, as the superstar signs autographs after an event.

Hit the Post

Postage stamps have been a part of Olympic celebrations since the very beginning, when Athens issued a series of stamps in 1896 to help offset the cost of hosting the first-ever Games sanctioned by the International Olympic Committee (IOC). Today, about 40 nations issue stamps for the Winter Games. Ice hockey has long been one of the favorite Winter Olympic events, and the popularity of hockey is demonstrated by the large number of postage stamps featuring hockey players issued by countries around the world, many of which do not even have Olympic hockey teams – or even participate in the Winter Games. Hockey sets are almost always among the first to fly off the post office shelves. Some rare and interesting examples can be viewed above and on pages 33 and 34.

One of the most collected American Olympic hockey stamps is the 15-cent issue featured at the top left; it commemorates the 1980 Games in Lake Placid, New York, and is part of a much larger set featuring other sports that are part of the Olympic Games. When new commemorative stamps go on sale, post offices around the word usually mark the occasion with a special First Day of Issue cancel. The envelopes shown here were specially printed with the words "First Day of Issue" and special designs, which make them even more desirable to collectors and hockey fans.

Orr POWER

▶ Bobby Orr flies through the air after scoring the 1969–70 Stanley Cup–winning goal 40 seconds into overtime of Game 4. The photograph of this moment is one of the sport's most iconic images, and would not be such had St. Louis Blues defenseman Noel Picard not tripped Orr, which he did moments after Orr slid the puck past Blues' goalie Glenn Hall.

▼ A Bobby Orr Power Play pinball machine and accompanying advertisement, featuring Orr as a Chicago Black Hawk (representing the United States) taking on Team Canada. Notice how Orr is illustrated on the game as a right-hand shot when in reality he shoots left.

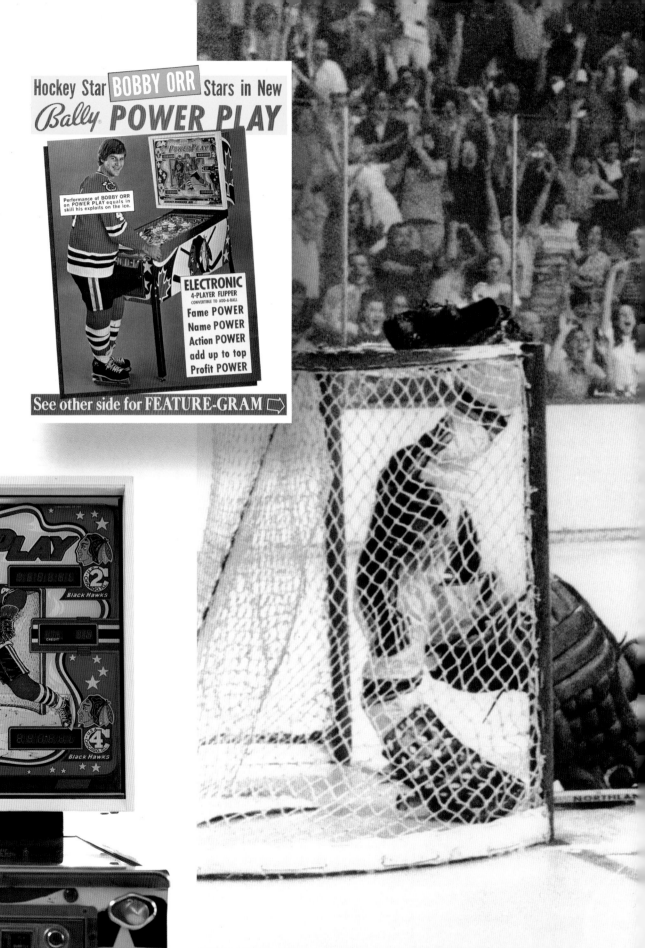

2 PLAYING

THE GAME

The Hockey Hall of Fame is filled to the brim with items that recall the heroics, inspirational plays, awe-inspiring achievements and legendary exploits that have happened on the rink – a collection of emotions and moments seared into the fabric of time and preserved for all to see. Of course, a museum can't actually exhibit an emotion or preserve a memory. Instead, hockey's hallowed halls exhibit items that offer hockey fans a way to relieve the emotion and vividly remember the game.

To see Guy Lafleur's No. 10 Montreal jersey is to remember his grace and speed – hair flying in the wind – as he streaked down the wing on those fabulous Canadiens teams of the 1970s. To view the carvings and tape job of the goal stick used by Percy LeSueur during the pre-NHL Cup-challenge days is to recall newsreel footage of old-time hockey and sepia photos of neatly groomed gentlemen who wowed fans with displays of speed and skill previously unmatched in sport. To gaze upon Sidney Crosby's "golden goal" Olympic puck is to remember the feeling of a nation rising to its feet in exalted joy while simultaneously exhaling a communal sigh of relief.

The magic and importance of the Hockey Hall of Fame is found in these items, which intersect personal and collective memory. The sticks, skates, pucks and masks shown in this chapter illustrate hockey's touchstone moments, obscure records, defunct leagues and Hall of Fame careers. They provide a window into the emotions and memories of playing the game and into those who played the game well.

◀ King Clancy's Toronto Maple Leafs jersey worn during the early 1930s.

▶ Boston Bruins jersey, circa 1974–76, worn by No. 4 Bobby Orr.

◀ Mark Messier's New York Rangers jersey from the 2000–01 season.

▶ Montreal Canadiens jersey, circa 1983, worn by Guy Lafleur toward the end of his time in Montreal.

◀ Detroit sweater, circa 1970, worn by Gordie Howe toward the end of his time with the Red Wings.

Sweater worn by Australia's Robin Dewhurst in Australia's IIHF debut at the 1960 Squaw Valley Games.

Harbin China's Heilongjiang Provincial Sport School jersey, circa 1974–82.

Denmark National Team sweater, circa 1978.

Bela Haray's Hungarian club-team sweater, 1935–36.

◄ Game-worn Japanese National Team sweater from the 1960 Squaw Valley Olympics.

Robbie Ftorek's Team USA jersey, worn during the inaugural Canada Cup tournament in 1976.

Canada vs the Russians

Canada and Russia have played each other many times on the world stage, and while their most famous meeting may be the Summit Series of 1972, Canadians and Russians had most definitely battled before that historic series. On the left is a photo from the late 1950s of a member of Canada's Whitby Dunlops scoring a goal against a Soviet club team. Notice how the Soviet players wear red while their goaltender wears blue. Above is an image taken during the 1974 Summit Series – a matchup similar to that of 1972, except Team Canada was made up of players from the WHA instead of the NHL. Team Canada lost that series to the Soviets 4–1–3.

Canada on the World Stage

Canada has a rich history of international competition. Pictured here are but a few Team Canada jerseys. To read more about the individual jerseys, see page 206.

▲ Official's sweater worn by Bill Stewart during the 1935–36 NHL season. Two seasons later, Stewart won the Stanley Cup as coach of the Chicago Black Hawks.

▶ **Whistles** *Top left*: Whistle used during Bill Friday's entire NHL career. In 1972–73 Friday jumped to the WHA, giving the league instant officiating credibility. *Far left*: Whistle used by Red Storey during his eight-year NHL career as a referee. *Middle*: Linesman Neil Armstrong's whistle from his final career game, his 1,744th, in 1978. *Top right*: Whistle used by referee John McCauley. McCauley became the NHL's referee-in-chief in 1986. *Bottom right*: Acme Thunderer referee whistle, circa 1935, used by Wilf Loughlin after retiring from his playing career in 1927.

Bells *Top*: Brass referee bell (circa 1925) used by Lou Marsh while officiating amateur and NHL games. The NHL used bells for a brief time, and Marsh may have used this bell during the New York Rangers' first franchise game, on November 16, 1926. *Bottom*: Bell used by Clarence Campbell early in his officiating career. Campbell would go on to become NHL president in 1946, holding the office for 31 years.

Skates *Top*: Skate used by linesman George Hayes during his 18-year NHL career, between 1946 and 1964.

Hayes was the first on-ice official to work 1,000 games. *Bottom*: Linesman Ray Scapinello wore this skate for his final season of officiating, in 2003–04. "Scampy" worked 2,500 regular-season games, a record for linesmen.

I.D. Badge Ray Scapinello's credentials from the final game of his career, Game 6 of the 2004 Stanley Cup final, between the Calgary Flames and the Tampa Bay Lightning. Tampa Bay forced Game 7 with a 3–2 double-overtime victory.

Boards End board from old Chicago Stadium.

All in a Day's Work

Often the object of ridicule and scorn, referees and linesmen are constantly in the line of fire – having to keep the peace and make the right call – and never get a shift off. On the left, linesman George Hayes is breaking up a fight between Boston and Toronto combatants. Above, referee Jyri Petteri Ronn is climbing the net for an aerial view of the goal line during a goalmouth scrum.

380-Toronto
2-MARS-1966
BUTS

McGill
REDMEN

OILERS

UNION
U
COLLEGE

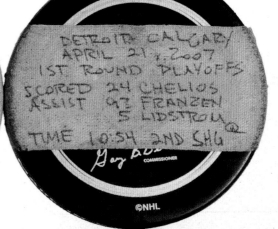

DETROIT CALGARY
APRIL 21, 2007
1ST ROUND PLAYOFFS
SCORED 24 CHELIOS
ASSIST 93 FRANZEN
5 LIDSTROM
TIME 10:54 2ND SHG

©NHL

MINNESOTA
NORTH STARS

718

In Glas Co

50
NATIONAL
HOCKEY LEAGUE
PUCK
CLINTON   COMETS
EHL

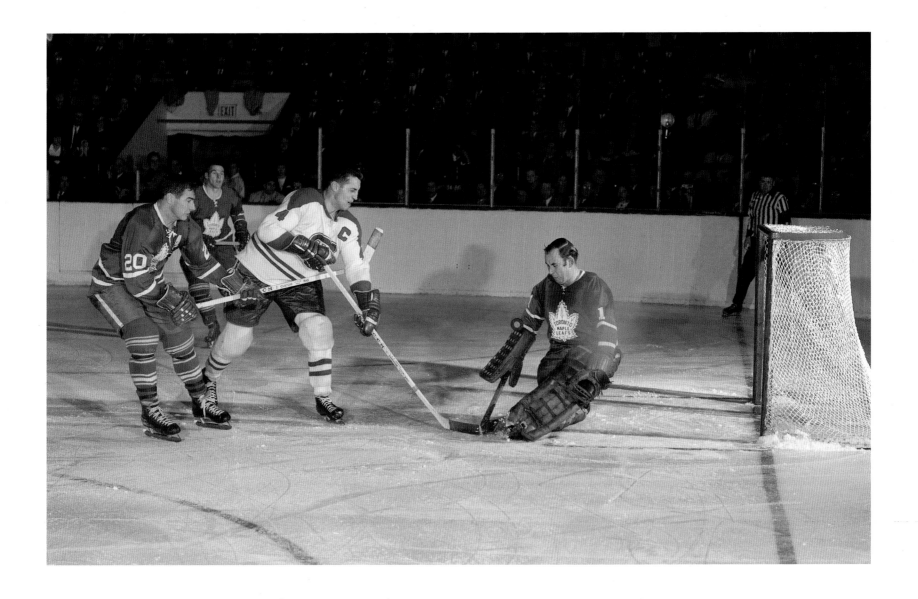

Big Béliveau

Captain Jean Béliveau powers his way through Bob Pulford to force a shot on Leafs goalie Bruce Gamble during the 1965–66 season. Béliveau scored his 380th career goal on Gamble later that season, during a 3–3 tie on March 2, 1966, at Maple Leaf Gardens. The goal placed the Canadiens captain one ahead of Ted Lindsay for third place on the NHL's all-time goal chart. The puck that Béliveau put behind Gamble can be seen at the top left corner of page 52. To read more about each puck, see page 206.

Mosie's Magic

The night of March 23, 1952, saw a record set at Madison Square Garden in New York that will likely never be broken.
Bill Mosienko of the Chicago Black Hawks fired these three pucks (left) past rookie goalie Lorne Anderson of the Rangers in
a span of 21 seconds. Coincidentally, teammate Gus Bodnar also set a record for the fastest three assists during the Hawks'
7–6 victory. Mosienko scored at 6:09 and 6:20, grabbing both pucks for posterity as his 29th and 30th goals of the year. Ten
seconds later he scored again, and in the excitement he had to be reminded by teammate Jimmy Peters to grab the record-
setting puck. Minutes later, "Mosie" almost scored a fourth time, ringing a shot off the post.

An assortment of side-labeled and game-used pucks from amateur, international and NHL play. Games include: the bronze-medal game of the 2009 World Championship, between Switzerland and the USA; the gold-medal game of the 2000 Royal Bank Cup, between the Fort McMurray Oil Barons and the Rayside-Balfour Sabrecats; the gold-medal game of the 2008 World Championship, between Canada and Russia; the NHL Challenge Stockholm 2000, between Djurgardens IF and the Vancouver Canucks; the gold-medal game of the 2006 Winter Olympics, between Finland and Sweden; the 2007 Western Hockey League final, between the Vancouver Giants and the Medicine Hat Tigers; the 2005 World Junior Championship final, between Russia and Canada; Game 6 of the 2008 Stanley Cup final, between Detroit and Pittsburgh; the 1999 Women's 3 Nations Cup final, between Canada and the USA; the 2004 World Women's Championship final, between Canada and the USA; Game 6 of the 2010 Stanley Cup final, between Philadelphia and Chicago; and one of the many used during "The Long Game," played in Newport, Nova Scotia, for 30 consecutive hours from January 4 to 5, 2002.

Tools of the Trade

A variety of sticks from professional, amateur and international play.

To read more about each stick, see page 207.

Poke Check

Goalie sticks used during professional, amateur and international competition. To read more about each stick, see page 207.

▲ New York Islanders sniper Mike Bossy scores his second goal against Quebec Nordiques goaltender John Grahame in a January 24, 1981, contest. The game was number 50 on the Islanders' schedule, and the goal, coming with less than two minutes left in the game, was Bossy's 50th of the season. The marker was a dream come true for Bossy, who had confided in friends earlier in the season that his aim was to tie the record of 50 goals in 50 games set by Maurice "Rocket" Richard in 1944–45. Only three other players have scored 50 goals in 50 games since: Wayne Gretzky, Mario Lemieux and Brett Hull.

◀ Stan Mikita is putting the finishing touches on a few of his "banana blade" sticks in the mid-1960s. Chicago's Mikita and Bobby Hull are credited with being the first two players to curve their sticks, changing the flight of the puck, and the game, dramatically.

19
McCLEISH
FIBERGLASS HANDLE
16
CHOUINARD
R.VAIVE
PATTERN MADE
P.M.P
19
RIGHT
BOSSY
GERRY COSBY & CO
HADFIELD
EASTON
EASTON
ULTRA
GLASS
B.CARPENTER
RIGHT
MC DONALD
CARSON
17
P.M.P 7000
FEATHER-BALANCED
FEATHER-BALANCED
P.M.P 7000
ROBITAILLE
20
FEATHER-BALANCED

Milestone Makers

Taped, curved and honed to perfection, the stick is the player's main tool. Like a slugger's bat or a fielder's glove, the stick is a hockey player's best friend. Pictured above and on the page opposite are examples of the magical happenings that can occur when a player and stick work together to achieve greatness. To read more about the sticks on these pages, see page 208.

Greatness Measured in Rubber, Aluminum and Leather
Wayne Gretzky has scored more goals and had more helpers than
any other player in NHL history. To the left are Gretzky's pucks
from his march to the all-time NHL points lead; he surpassed
Gordie Howe's remarkable total of 1,850 points on October 15,
1989. Counting down, left-to-right, and starting on the top row
are pucks 1,851; 1,850; 1,849; 1,848; 1,847; 1,846; 1,845; 1,844
and 1,843. Above are Gretzky's gloves, stick and helmet, as well
as the puck he scored with and the net he scored in at LA's Forum
on March 23, 1994. The goal was Gretzky's 802nd, making him the
NHL's all-time leading scorer and breaking another Gordie Howe
record previously thought unassailable.

Soft Hands

An assortment of gloves from all levels of play. To read more about each pair, see page 209.

Gloves worn by Detroit's Gordie Howe during the 1952–53 season. Howe captured his third of four straight Art Ross Trophies by posting 95 points, and he was voted to his second straight Hart Trophy.

◄ Purple-and-gold gloves worn by Glenn Goldup of the Los Angeles Kings in 1980–81, his final full NHL season.

► Washington's Mike Gartner wore these gloves in 1984–85 to record his only 50-goal, 100-point season. Gartner reached both milestones with a two-goal, two-assist performance in a 7–2 victory over Pittsburgh on April 7, 1985.

◄ Gloves worn by Team Canada's Jean Ratelle during the 1972 Summit Series versus the USSR. Ratelle scored four points in six games.

► Green Bay Gamblers gloves worn by Anders Lee throughout the 2009–10 United States Hockey League season and playoffs. Lee led all playoff scorers with 22 points and was named playoff MVP as the Gamblers won the Clark Cup.

This Is Our House!

Bricks and mortar taken from various renovated and demolished arenas. *Top left:* A brown brick from the Civic Arena in Pittsburgh, also known as "The Igloo," home to the Pittsburgh Penguins from 1967 to 2010. *Middle left:* Two bricks bound by mortar from Toronto's Mutual Street Arena, home to Toronto's Blueshirts, Arenas, St. Patrick's and Maple Leafs; replaced by Maple Leaf Gardens in 1931. *Top right:* Two bricks from the Detroit Olympia, the Red Wings' home from 1927 to 1979, when the Joe Louis Arena opened. *Middle right:* A pale brick from the famed Chicago Stadium, home of the Blackhawks. The stadium hosted its last game on April 28, 1994. *Bottom:* A gray slab of flooring removed from the Rochester War Memorial Auditorium during renovations throughout 1998–99. The War Memorial opened in 1955 and is still operating.

THE PRODIGAL SON
Loving Hockey, Leaving It and Coming Home

| **DON GILLMOR**

Stop me if you've heard this one: As a boy I used to leave my house in the dark and walk to the rink and put on my skates in the player's box then play hockey by myself, calling out my heroics in a play-by-play voice learned from Foster Hewitt's final years, waiting until the next boy arrived and a game would start. Others would arrive in the hesitant dawn, and I remember every day being cold, bright and windless. The game evolved as the day went on and more players arrived, players of different ages and skill levels and pugnacity. Like the Roman Empire, it grew from barely connected villages into a mighty entity that was fast and dangerous, and then it slowly collapsed, 10 hours later, as people finally left for dinner, called home by older sisters, collected by fathers. The game went on after the lights were turned off and the clubhouse was locked up, a handful of us playing in the dark until someone was hit in the face and we walked him home, weeping, and presented him to his outraged mother.

My story and thousands like it are part of the fabric of the idyllic Canadian childhood. It is a mythic and familiar story that could be transplanted to any number of towns across the nation. I lived for hockey, and the reasons I eventually left the game were sown during these early years.

The majority of my youth hockey career was played as a member of the Wildwood Warriors, the smallest community team in Winnipeg, Manitoba. So tiny was our community that we had trouble finding enough kids to put a team on the ice. We lost almost every game.

We did beat a private boys' school that had students from England and the Middle East who were dismissed locally as uniform-wearing nancies. It was one of the few games I looked forward to. They had kids who had never seen ice outside of a drinking glass and who still walked on their skates. We beat them 6–0. Afterward they came into our dressing room, introduced themselves with handshakes and poured us all hot chocolate from a large steel tankard. We felt they didn't really understand the game.

Our most critical game was against a team of girls, a match arranged by our coach and billed as a morale-booster, though I suspect it was born out of a bet against their female coach. They were, in memory, bigger than we were. Their captain was 13, a year older than me, and a fearsome tomboy who had impressive hockey skills – a rarity in those pre–Hayley Wickenheiser days – and who made adolescent boys wary because there was a good chance she could beat them up. After two periods the game was still scoreless. Our coach began calling us by feminine derivatives of our names (Joan for John, Donna for Don, etc.) and wondered aloud how long we would carry this disgrace if we lost. ("Forever" was his opinion.) In the third period I broke the scoreless tie – backhand, top shelf – rescuing us from this final ignominy.

This stirring victory didn't help us against the rest of the league though, nor did it help my desire to play organized hockey. We continued to get thrashed weekly, and after a while I began to dread the games. I lived for shinny, where my true hockey soul was released: I could fly down the ice and experiment with new moves and call out my own greatness in Hewitt's distinctive tone. In a game of shinny there are few worries about being on the losing side because the sides change as new players arrive. The weak side can easily pick up a deadly sniper, and with a few quick ones everything is equal again.

In Winnipeg the off-season could be short, but I occupied my time by collecting trading cards and playing ball hockey, which, like shinny, provided welcome relief from losing actual games. Gordie Howe was my idol, and I read his book *Hockey … Here's Howe!*, which had a Norman Rockwell-like painting on the cover of Howe dropping the puck between two boys wearing Red Wings jerseys with his No. 9. I saw him play once, while visiting my cousin in Minneapolis. It was a big event. The Red Wings were in town playing the North Stars, and whenever Gordie was on the ice, I watched him rather than the play, hoping to see the secret to his magic, or at least see those famous elbows in action.

But despite the shinny, the ball hockey, the trading cards and the books, those losing seasons eventually took their toll.

When I was 15 I felt I'd had all the losing I could stand. Adolescence contained enough dread without adding that weekly drubbing. I abandoned the Wildwood Warriors and tried out for a neighboring community's team, a civic powerhouse that was routinely in the hunt for a championship. I made the team but my joy was short-lived. We stumbled through the season, losing more than we won. Once more, every team we faced seemed larger, more rigorously coached, more professional. Even the next day's shinny couldn't mitigate this disappointment. I was a skilled player, I loved the game and it was in my blood, but I felt the game had somehow betrayed me.

I quit.

I bought a second-hand pair of Head Standard skis at a sale organized by the guy who delivered our bread, and the following year, instead of heading to the rink that was 150 feet from our house, I headed for the unironically named Mount Agassiz. It was not the mountain of the same name located just outside Vancouver; instead, it was a bump on the prairie three hours

north of Winnipeg that had straw sticking out from the snow and temperatures of –13°F (–25°C). There was a rope tow that was run by a tractor engine and operated by an old, very grumpy farmer.

After a season on the slopes of rural Manitoba, the hockey/skiing divide was further cemented when my family moved to Calgary. I bought a season pass at a bigger mountain and scheduled all my university classes for Mondays, Wednesdays and Fridays so I could ski Tuesdays and Thursdays (as well as during the weekend). The Flames hadn't moved from Atlanta to Calgary yet, the World Hockey Association was muddying the pro hockey waters and the Crazy Canucks were emerging on the international ski scene. Hockey became a distant memory.

In the 1980s I moved to Montreal, home to the hockey team that I'd cheered for as a child (Gordie may have been God, but the Red Wings were fallible). I went with a friend to see the Canadiens at the fabled Forum, where they were playing the Leafs no less. We had seats that were pressed against the glass in one of the ends. As the players wheeled by, or crashed into the glass in front of us, their faces twisted in surprise or pain, I was suddenly reminded of the extraordinary physics of the game, the speed of

Champagne and sparkling wine used during a variety of championship celebrations in professional and international play. *Top row, left to right*: Russian sparkling wine consumed by Team Russia after winning the 2003 World Junior Championship; Tott's champagne used in celebration by Pat Verbeek of the Dallas Stars after winning the Stanley Cup on June 19, 1999; the ECHL's Mississippi Sea Wolves celebrated with this champagne after winning the 1999 Kelly Cup; sparkling wine with which the Canadian women's team celebrated their gold-medal victory at the 2002 Olympics. *Bottom row, left to right*: Victory bottle of champagne consumed by the 2008 Stanley Cup–champion Detroit Red Wings; "Canadian Champagne" used by the Hull Olympiques to celebrate their 1997 Memorial Cup win; sparkling wine consumed by Team Canada after capturing gold in men's hockey at the 2010 Olympics; champagne enjoyed by the Central Hockey League's Huntsville Channel Cats after their 1999 Levins Cup victory; champagne consumed by the 2009 Stanley Cup–champion Pittsburgh Penguins.

Even hockey socks can tell a story. *Left to right*: Terry Sawchuk's socks, used during his second stint with the Detroit Red Wings, from 1957 to 1964; Sawchuck led the league in starts (70) his first season back in the red and white. Socks worn by Billy Trew of the Western Professional Hockey League's El Paso Buzzards for the 1996–97 season; the team claimed their second consecutive league championship. Socks worn by Hilda Ranscombe of the Preston Rivulettes, winners of six women's national championships, during the 1930s. Royal Canadian Air Force socks belonging to team trainer George McFaul when the club won gold as Canada's hockey representatives at the 1948 Olympics.

the players, the velocity of the puck and the impossibility of those high-speed maneuvers. It was thrilling.

A few weeks later, my friend invited me to play shinny at the rink in Westmount Park. I had to borrow skates and a stick. The game was wild and fun. A fight broke out, and since I was the closest thing to an adult on the ice, I went over to break it up, using what I felt was a Larry Robinson–like moral presence backed up by size. I played a few more times and began watching the Canadiens regularly on TV. Like Michael Corleone in *The Godfather,* I could feel myself being slowly sucked back into the national business.

Years later I moved to Toronto and bought a house that was, by curious coincidence, exactly the same distance from a hockey rink as my childhood home had been, not an easy thing to do in that rink-starved town. At night I could hear the distinctive sounds of pucks echoing off the boards, and I found it comforting.

I started a family and did my duty as a parent and taught my children how to skate, bent over and holding them up and skating in that Quasimodo posture for what seemed like a hundred hours. The slow march back to hockey turned a corner when I sent my son Cormac to hockey camp and then enrolled him in a league. I joined that grim parade of exhausted-looking parents who show up for early morning games on the weekend with their newspapers and coffee. I watched Cormac struggle with the rest of the five-year-olds, all of them skating choppily after the puck like lemmings.

My son could walk to the end of the street and into the park and join the shinny game the way I had as a boy. Only a few hours a week were set aside for kids' shinny, and it wasn't unusual to have 50 people on the ice at the same time. It was an exercise in chaos. I joined him in these games, recalling the shinny of my youth. Perhaps they'd been chaotic as well, though in gilded memory there were six aside and I stickhandled among them like Orr in his prime.

Cormac progressed through summer skills camps and house leagues, and I would watch and find myself yelling increasingly specific instructions, none of which could be heard past the glass in the arena. I noticed I was yelling many of the same things my mother had yelled at me when I had played. My son skated the way I had

and played the way I had, with more finesse than grit perhaps, and I was telling him to go into the corners, to move up to the point. There were mornings when I felt I was watching a home movie of myself playing; it was a curious, nostalgic experience.

When Cormac was nine, I was offered a chance to coach his team, and I thought, "Why not? Now I wouldn't have to yell over the glass at least."

My first fear was that history would repeat itself and we would be marooned on a weak team and go through a season of mounting loss that would scar us both. But the world had changed since I had played. For one thing, teams are balanced to avoid blowouts. If that isn't enough, there is a limit to how many goals a player can score, limiting the dominance of one brilliant player to a hat trick. And if all else fails, the scoreboard only registers a five-goal differential, regardless of what the actual score is. Coaching styles have changed as well. The Punch Imlach beat-'em-in-the-alley philosophy that had filtered down to Pee Wee when I was a boy is anathema now. We can't tell them, as I was told as an eight-year-old, to tear the opponent's heart out and spit in the hole.

My co-coach made the Walter Gretzky–like sacrifice of icing his backyard, and our sons spend hours there, playing keep-away, practicing tricks, raising the puck into the battered cedar fence. They talk of their hockey heroes and relive the game they've just played; they eat their lunch standing up in their skates and map their futures in the NHL.

The circle of my return to hockey was fully closed when I recently went shopping for hockey equipment, ready to play once more. It helps that Ontario's skiing isn't much more glamorous than Manitoba's. I've retained my wariness of girl's teams, especially in this modern Wickenheiser era, but I'm ready to face a private boys' school, or their teachers at least. As former Toronto Maple Leaf Ken Wregget said, "Hockey is like a disease, you can't shake it."

DON GILLMOR is an award-winning journalist and the author of *Canada: A People's History* and *Kanata*.

Blades of Steel

Legendary Toronto Maple Leafs equipment manager Tommy Naylor inspects skates in 1960. To the left are skates used by players in the NHL, IHL and CHL. *From left to right*: Battered skates worn by Dallas' Craig Ludwig for the 1998–99 season, including Dallas' Stanley Cup victory; Micron Megas worn by Doug Wickenheiser of the IHL's Fort Wayne Komets before his retirement from pro hockey in 1994; the Central Hockey League's 2006–07 Most Outstanding Defenseman, Brad Williamson, wore these skates as his Colorado Eagles won the 2007 CHL final; skates worn by Wayne Gretzky during one of his three seasons with the New York Rangers.

Kaleidoscopes of skates. To read more about the four featured skates above and on the facing page, see page 210.

New York Rangers defenseman Brian Leetch wore these heavily reinforced skates from 1989 to 1995. Throughout those six seasons, Leetch earned his first Norris Trophy (1992) and, while leading the Rangers to the 1994 Stanley Cup title, became the first U.S.-born player to win the Conn Smythe Trophy.

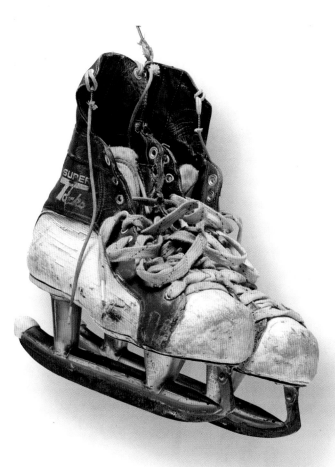

◀ California Golden Seals skates worn by Morris Mott from 1972 to 1974. Introduced by owner Charles Finlay, the skates were scrapped in the 1973–74 season, when the club was taken over by the NHL.

▶ Skates worn by Dickie Boon from 1899 to 1905. Boon won the Stanley Cup in 1902 and 1903 with the Montreal Amateur Athletic Association.

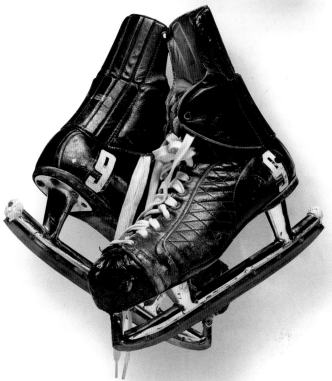

◀ Skates worn by Sepp Puschinig of Klagenfurter AC for the 1968–69 Austrian Hockey League season.

▶ The skates Gordie Howe wore for his final few years with Detroit, ending in 1971. Howe laced up for the WHA in 1973, retiring for good in 1979–80, at age 52.

Hartford Whalers pants worn by defenseman Brad Shaw from 1989–90 to 1991–92. Shaw made the NHL's All-Rookie Team following the 1989–90 season.

◄ Knee brace used by Buffalo's Dave Andreychuk.

► Shoulder pads worn by Dallas' Jere Lehtinen during the 1998–99 season, including the club's triple-overtime Stanley Cup victory, during which he scored a goal and assisted on the game winner.

◄ Doug Bentley of the Chicago Black Hawks wore these pants during the 1948–49 NHL season, when he was named a Second All-Star Team center.

► Anaheim's Teemu Selänne wore these elbow pads throughout the 2006–07 season, helping the Ducks capture the franchise's first Stanley Cup.

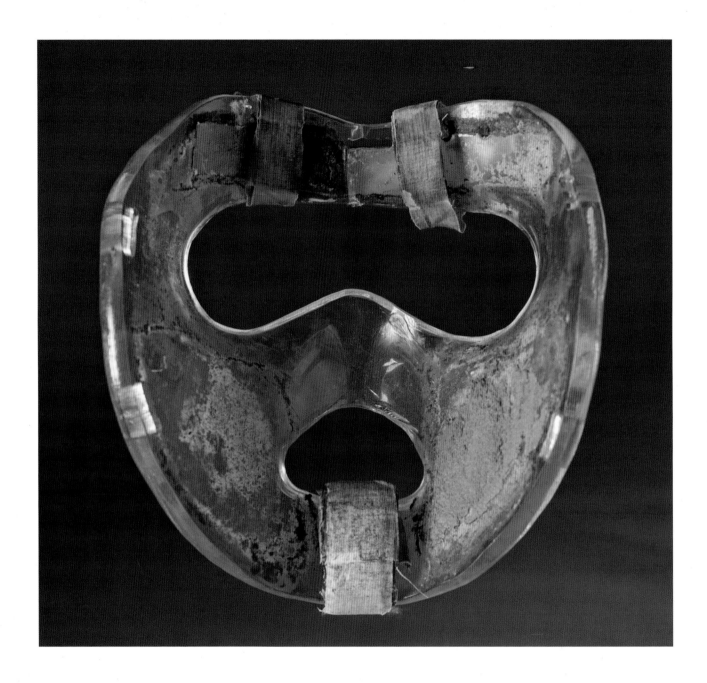

The Masked Man

Right: Jacques Plante in the Montreal Canadiens' dressing room in the late 1950s wearing a clear Plexiglas-like mask that only ever saw action in practice, as coach Toe Blake thought it would impede Plante's play in a game. *Above:* A view of the mask, minus its foam cushioning, from the inside. Early in the 1959–60 season, Plante changed the face of hockey by becoming the first goalie to wear a mask regularly in NHL action.

The Changing Face of Hockey
A close-up view of the mask Jacques
Plante used on November 1, 1959,
to protect his face upon returning to
action after a 21-minute delay to close
a gash incurred by an Andy Bathgate
backhand. Plante insisted that, from
that moment, he would only continue to
play if he was allowed to wear his mask.

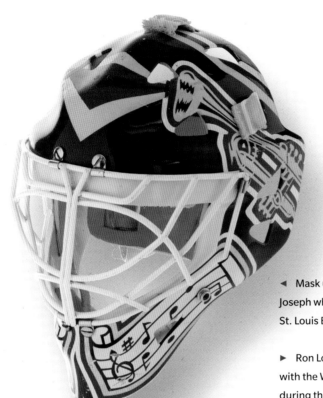

◄ Mask used by Curtis "Cujo" Joseph while playing for the St. Louis Blues in the early 1990s.

► Ron Low's mask from his time with the Washington Capitals, during the mid-1970s.

◄ Terry Sawchuk began wearing this mask during the 1962–63 season, but not before his face was crisscrossed by the scars of more than 350 stitches.

► Pelle Lindbergh donned this mask for the majority of his all-too-brief NHL career, during which he earned the 1984–85 Vezina Trophy.

Detroit Red Wings pants worn by netminder Eddie Giacomin while wrapping up his Hall of Fame career with nine games at the start of the 1977–78 NHL season.

◄ The pants Jim Craig wore while backstopping the 1980 U.S. Olympic team to hockey gold – and most famously during the 4–3 "Miracle on Ice" victory over the Soviets.

► Pittsburgh's Marc-André Fleury wore this combination chest-and-arms protector throughout the 2006–07 NHL season, during which he posted a career-best 40 wins.

◄ Black-and-brown leather CCM goalie skates worn by Jacques Plante of the WHA's Edmonton Oilers during his last season of play, 1974–75.

► Skates worn by Ed Belfour of the Dallas Stars, circa 2000. Belfour spent five seasons with the Stars and backstopped the team to their 1999 Stanley Cup.

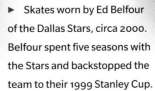

The Ambidextrous Goalie

Bill Durnan played seven seasons in the NHL, from 1943 to 1950, all for the Montreal Canadiens. He led the league in goals-against average and was named to the First All-Star Team and won the Vezina Trophy in all but one of those seasons. Durnan's pads, stick and gloves from his time with Montreal are shown on the right. The gloves are particularity special – as demonstrated in this action photo of Durnan – as he could use the ambidextrous mitts like a blocker to hold his stick and direct pucks away or like a catcher to trap pucks. The mesh in the background belongs to another Hab's great, Patrick Roy, who cut it from the net he defended as a member of the Colorado Avalanche when he recorded his 448th career victory, surpassing the NHL's all-time wins leader, Terry Sawchuk.

Terry Sawchuk, shown here swatting a puck out of harm's way as a member of the Detroit Red Wings in the early 1950s, wore the pads on the left during his second stint with the Wings, which lasted from 1957 to 1964. In all, Sawchuk played parts of 14 NHL seasons with Detroit over three separate stops, playing with Boston, Toronto, Los Angeles and New York when not in Motown. His 447 wins stand as the third most of all time.

Johnny Bower's battle-worn pads from his Cup-winning years in Toronto in the 1960s. Notice the lack of vertical bar on the outside of the knee.

The last pair of goalie pads worn by Philadelphia's Pelle Lindbergh. He used them for the start of the 1985–86 season, before he died tragically in a car accident.

Corey Hirsch's Team Canada pads, worn for the 1994 Winter Olympics. Canada finished second after a 3–2 shoot-out loss to Sweden in the gold-medal game.

The pads Sami Jo Small wore during the 2000 Women's World Championship. Canada won gold and Small was named the tournament's top goalie.

The Wall

Pads stacked in the butterfly position, the principle technique used in modern goaltending. To read more about each set, see page 210.

The gloves Nikolai Khabibulin wore while backstopping the Tampa Bay Lightning to the Stanley Cup in 2003–04. Khabibulin posted a .933 save percentage, a 1.71 goals-against average and five shutouts over 23 playoff games.

▲ Gloves worn by Jessie Vetter of the University of Wisconsin Badgers in 2006–07. She was named a First Team All-American and the Frozen Four All-Tournament Team goaltender.

▲ Phoenix's Brian Boucher set an NHL modern-era record of 332:01 minutes of goal-less hockey with these gloves, from December 31, 2003, to January 9, 2004.

▲ Trapper and blocker belonging to goaltender Tom Barrasso. He wore them during his final 10 games with the Buffalo Sabres, in 1988–89.

▲ Ed Chadwick of the Buffalo Bisons wore these leather gloves in the American Hockey League during the mid- to late-1960s.

The Brotherhood of Goaltenders

It has often been said that to play goal takes a special temperament. Above, Eddie Giacomin of the New York Rangers rests in a moment of in-game solitude as he gazes down the ice, readying himself for the next instance of frenzied action. To the right, George Hainsworth and Roy Worters shake hands on April 2, 1936, after Hainsworth's Leafs had downed Worters' Americans 3–1 in the final game of the Stanley Cup semifinals. Andy Lytle of the *Toronto Star* reported that Worters' hand was shaking so much he cold barely hold his cigarette – an illustration of how nerve-racking and dangerous goaltending was at the time.

Yves Bélanger, Atlanta Flames,
1978–79.

Murray Bannerman, Chicago Black Hawks,
mid-1980s.

Ed Belfour, Chicago Blackhawks,
mid-1990s.

Jon Casey, Minnesota North Stars,
early 1990s.

Mike Palmateer, Toronto Maple Leafs,
late 1970s.

Bob Essensa, Winnipeg Jets,
early 1990s.

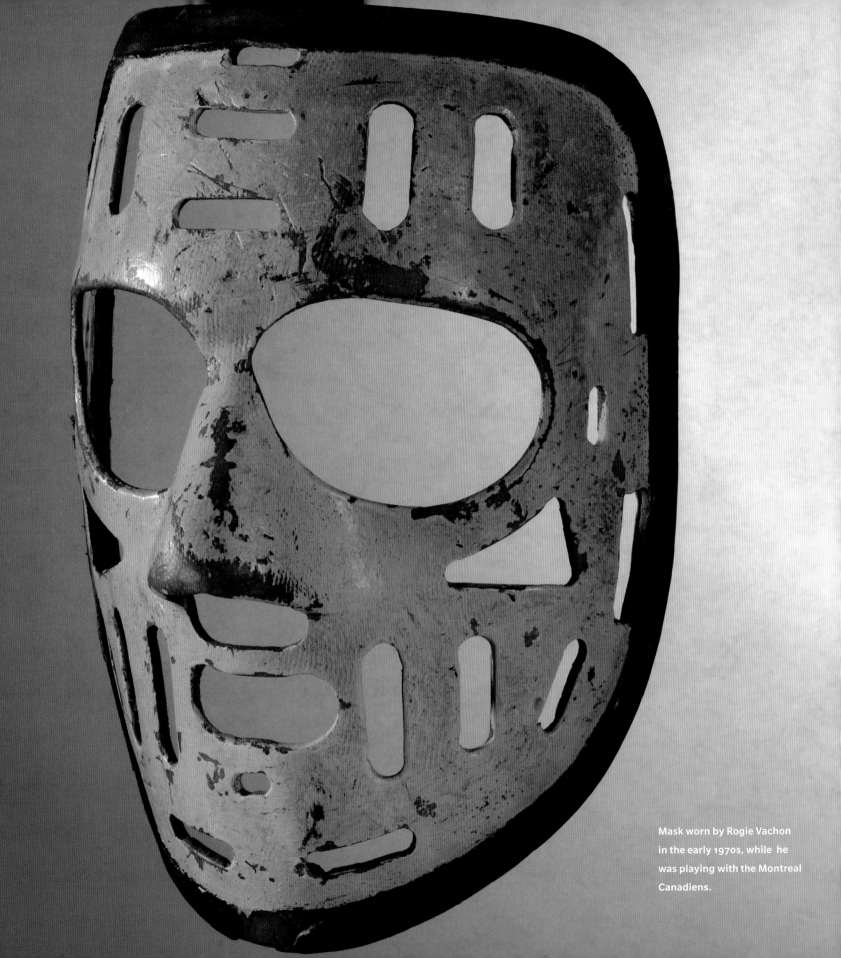

Mask worn by Rogie Vachon in the early 1970s, while he was playing with the Montreal Canadiens.

Ace Bailey and Eddie Shore shake hands in Boston on March 6, 1934. It was the first time Toronto star Bailey had been to Boston Garden since December 12, 1933, when he was upended by Shore, suffering a cerebral hemorrhage that ended his career and nearly killed him. Bailey absolved Shore of any wrongdoing, explaining that he felt the hit was part of the game. The NHL played an All-Star Game on February 14, 1934, raising over $20,000 for Bailey and his family. As a result of the incident, Shore wore a helmet for the rest of his career; on the right is one of Shore's helmets from this time.

◄ Trademark helmet worn by Denis Potvin of the New York Islanders throughout a good portion of his career, during the late 1970s and early 1980s.

► Boston Bruins helmet worn by Cam Neely throughout the majority of his 10 seasons with the Bruins.

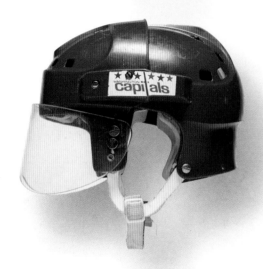

◄ Helmet worn by Mike Gartner during his time with the Washington Capitals (1979–88). Gartner was one of the first star players to permanently dawn a visor.

► Soviet forward Alexander Yakushev's hemlet, worn during the 1972 Summit Series. Yakushev scored seven goals and 11 points to lead the USSR in scoring.

◄ Red plastic and leather helmet, circa 1960s, worn by Bob McKenna of Boston University's junior varsity team during the 1971–72 season.

► Arkansas River Blades center Buddy Smith wore this "x-ray" helmet while representing the Southern Conference during the 2003 ECHL All-Star Game.

Cam Neely in action for the Boston Bruins in the early 1990s. Neely holds three Boston team records: career playoff goals (55), career power-play goals (24) and most goals in a season by a right wing (55), set in 1988–89.

Dressing-room Diversity
Paraphernalia from men's and women's international competition. To read more about each stall, see page 211.

NHL superstar Wayne Gretzky used this equipment
bag and associated gear in his final NHL game,
on April 18, 1999.

THE HIGHWAYS OF HOCKEY

| DAVE BIDINI

There are lines in life, but you can't see them. Because you can't see them, you cross them, and when you cross them, you find yourself in different places playing familiar games. At least, that's how it was for me in the early part of the 21st century, when I followed hockey to its cousin nations, including Russia, which I visited three times last decade.

I traveled to Russia once in the summer and again in the winter, both times as part of a film crew for my second "hocku-mentary," *The Hockey Nomad Goes to Russia*. In the combined two months, we rolled over some 2,500 miles (4,000 km) east to west, from St. Petersburg to Kazan to Moscow to the Altai Mountains, finding ice in Siberian church courtyards, abandoned Tatar factories and on the frozen wheat fields of the Russian breadbasket. We arrived to rink-side gold-toothed accordion players and left, hours later, to the weary thump of whatever discotheque had recently opened in town. Returning to our hotel rooms – in Kazan it was an art-deco high-rise, in Barnaul, a converted Soviet block apartment – we would receive call after call from hotel lobby concubines who considered us an easy mark. In Omsk, our film's director, Mike Downie, fielded a call from yet another person wanting something: it was NHL lockout star Brad Richards, who, during the NHL's labor stoppage, had signed on to play for Ak Bars Kazan of the Russian Superleague. At the centreman's request, Mike smuggled him a few cans of beer, forbidden by Kazan coach Diniyar Bilyaletdinov, the former Russian national.

My first trip to Omsk, the capital city of Siberia, happened in the golden light of the summer. Boulevardiers and young skirted women belied whatever impression I'd had of the place as some god-awful iceberg of despair. It was a broad city of rivers and bridges and chic thoroughfares on the cusp of Western-style decadence. Omsk in the summer was mostly a soccer city, but through falling snow and seizing cold a few months later, hockey returned to its rightful place as the region's number-one sport. The most popular team was the Omsk Avangard, captained by Jaromir Jagr.

Come December, outdoor skating was as much a part of city life as the clunking Soviet-era buses that filled the thoroughfares or the ubiquitous canopied liquor stands that lined the streets and remained open all hours. (Struck with insomnia early one weekday morning, I awoke at 4 a.m. to find a huddle of people gathered below my hotel window in sub-zero temperatures drinking whatever the bedraggled liquor stand proprietor was serving.)

In Omsk, we spent most of our time with the Kuznetsovs, a family of three who were still mourning their eldest son, who had been murdered during May Day celebrations in Chelyabinsk, their hometown. The Kuznetsov's youngest son, Genia, or Evgeny, was a hockey prodigy who'd been cherry-picked for the Omsk junior team, the Avangard. He was 13 and showed promise: he was a strong skater with a long stride and a good, heavy shot. His parents watched over and protected him in the shadow of their eldest son's death.

The Kuznetsovs lived in a small apartment on the edge of Omsk, which the team provided for them. Genia's father did odd jobs for the club, driving an official here, moving a bag of pylons there, while his mother, a sad-faced but classically beautiful

Russian woman, tended carefully to their home. Meeting her for the first time, she came armed with scrapbooks documenting Genia's progress through peewee hockey in Chelyabinsk, the site of one of Russia's early nuclear accidents and where, as recently as 2001, hepatitis B had been found in the water. After their move to Omsk, the Kuznetsovs were hopeful for their young son's future. Sitting on the edge of his small bed in his small room on a cold and sunny afternoon, Genia nervously threaded his fingers together before looking up and telling me, "My brother was a referee, and he taught me everything about the game. It is my wish to become a pro hockey player so that, one day, I can hold a tournament in my hometown dedicated to his memory."

The Omsk hockey community was largely supportive of Genia's airlift into their town, even though it meant that the young star absorbed a roster spot that, before, would have gone to one of the local boys. One morning, we met with four local hockey moms (three of them named Svetlana, and another named Tatiana), who expressed no objection to bringing in a kid who, ultimately, would improve their sons' team's fortunes. After coffees and cakes and some grousing about the responsibilities familiar to hockey parents everywhere – early mornings, long and boring drives, expensive team fees – one of their husbands brought us into the wood-paneled living room, where he opened a map of the former Soviet Union on the coffee table. There, he measured by thumb and forefinger the old nation's landmass, including bordering nations that had since gained independence.

"We were once so huge, so great," he told us, shaking his head. "We were probably the mightiest nation on Earth."

After hearing his words from another room, his son, who was in his mid-30s, came in and said, "Sure, Dad, but that was before. This Russia doesn't exist anymore."

"That is a great shame," said the father.

"Yes, but also no," said the son. "Before, if you had a problem with your boss at work, you could not complain. If you complained, you went to prison, to the gulags."

The father scoffed. "There were no gulags. This is only a rumor that the West spread around," he said.

"Father, you can go out there and see them. Of course they existed," said the son.

The father barked something in Russian and the room fell silent. The son left the room.

"So mighty, so strong," said the old man, muttering to himself as he closed the map.

After hanging around the Avangard's charming 8,000-seat home rink – which has since been razed in favor of a glassy monolith built with local oil money – we met a bunch of young fans who immediately accepted us into their fold. After finding out that we'd traveled from Canada, they forced sweaters, scarves and Avangard membership cards on us, demanding that we have them as keepsakes from our trip. In the end, we returned everything to them except an autographed fan club card with signatures scribbled on the back. (I still carry this around in my back pocket.) When I asked them about the gulags, they rolled their eyes and said that, "Whether they existed or not, the Soviet Union is still alive in people's minds."

One fellow, Tatan, told me that he'd had his head smashed in by local police after staging an Omsk fan rally in the parking lot before a game. It was the first gathering of its kind, and it drew suspicion in a community that, according to the young fans, was

---

Steve Yzerman's equipment bag from his final NHL season, 2005–06. It holds: elbow pads used by Adam Foote of the Quebec Nordiques for the 1994–95 season, as well as shoulder pads used by his Quebec teammate Curtis Leschyshyn; Gary Roberts' shin pads, used from 2003 to 2008, while playing for Toronto, Florida and Pittsburgh; Northland "Stan Mikita" helmet belonging to an unknown Toronto Maple Leaf; socks worn by Ron Francis during the 2001–02 season and pants worn by Craig Muni of the Buffalo Sabres during the 1994–95 season. Outside the bag sit skates worn by Toronto's Norm Ullman, gloves worn by St. Louis' Bernie Federko during the 1988–89 season, and the stick used by Luc Robitaille of the LA Kings to assist on Wayne Gretzky's 802nd career goal.

still very slow to change. Tatan told us that he still had headaches, but that the attack hadn't lessened his allegiance to the team.

"They are all I have here in Omsk," he said. "To us, the team and the players are everything. And even if the police try and stop us from singing and partying and carrying on, we will keep supporting them."

We watched Genia practice and play every day. There were times when he seemed to score at will, swooping around the ice as though the puck was taped to the end of his stick. After a tournament where he'd been named MVP, his prize was a cassette player/clock radio, we asked Genia if he was looking forward to an upcoming game against Chelyabinsk, who were in the same junior division as Omsk. He told us that it would be good to go home, but that playing against his friends would be hard. A lot of his schoolmates were now rival players, and they relished the opportunity to beat the team that had poached Genia. In the game, Genia ended up taking three minor penalties and was held off the score sheet. He left the ice slamming his stick and, afterward, seemed on the verge of tears. Despite his natural gifts, I wondered whether or not he possessed the maturity and resolve required to fight his way through Russian hockey, to say nothing of climbing the prospect ladder for a shot at the national junior team or, later, the NHL draft. Knowing that, in most cases, the promise of young athletes ends up unfulfilled, it was almost too sad to imagine the Kuznetsovs returning to Chelyabinsk, where an uncertain and difficult life fraught with the memory of their murdered son awaited them.

Ron Francis' equipment bag from his time with the Hartford Whalers (1981–82 to 1990–91) holds pants worn by Quebec's Joe Sakic during the 1994–95 season. Brad Richards' Tampa Bay Lightning gloves and Scott Niedermayer's Anaheim helmet from their respective Conn Smythe–winning playoff campaigns (2004 and 2007) sit on the bench. In the cubbies are elbow pads worn by New Jersey's Ken Daneyko during the 2000 playoffs, socks worn by Ching Johnson of the New York Americans during the 1937–38 season and skates worn by Clark Gillies of the New York Islanders during the 1985–86 season. Beside the bench are sticks used by Stan Mikita and Phil Esposito.

When we were leaving Omsk for the last stop on our Russian hockey tour, Barnaul, we arrived late at the train station. Running to our compartment, we passed a gold-plated car being swabbed and mopped by kerchiefed babushkas in old winter boots. I wondered aloud what it might take to ride in such opulence, and Yulia, our translator, said that, in Soviet times, the car had been reserved for high-ranking members of the Politburo loath to ride with the proletariat. As we reached our car at the end of the train, the conductor grunted and waved us back. Yulia asked him if there was a problem with our tickets, but it wasn't anything like that. Instead, he told us that the gold car had been reserved for us.

During hockey season, it's hard not to think about my travels to Russia. It doesn't take much. Over Christmas 2010, I tuned in to watch the Russian junior team play Switzerland at the World Junior Championship in Buffalo. It was a dull game, played over the holidays in the middle of the afternoon. Then, announcer Gord Miller said something that caught my ear. At first, I wasn't sure what I'd I heard. Then, he said it again: "Kuznetsov." I rose out of my chair to listen more closely. "Kuznetsov." I waited to hear the player's first name, but it never came. In the second period, the camera zoomed in on the player's face, and I could see that it was him. The announcer said, "He's from Chelyabinsk, where he relocated after a few years playing in Omsk."

There was the same long stride, the same mop of blonde hair, the same heavy shot. It turned out that the Washington Capitals had drafted him to the NHL in the first round. Later, he would lead the Russian charge to defeat Canada in the World Junior Championship final, helping his team score five unanswered goals to win the tournament. Genia would be named to the tournament All-Star team. The kid from Chelyabinsk had come a long way.

DAVE BIDINI, the Hockey Nomad, is a musician, journalist and author. He was a founding member of the acclaimed rock band the Rheostatics and has written several books, including *Tropic of Hockey* and *Home and Away: In Search of Dreams at the Homeless World Cup of Soccer.*

▲ Toronto Maple Leafs equipment handler Tim Daly is surrounded by heavy-duty travel cases outside of Maple Leaf Gardens in the 1930s.

▶ Grant Fuhr's equipment bag from the 1999–2000 season. It holds: pants worn by Carolina's Eric Staal for the 2005–06 season, including Carolina's Stanley Cup victory; shin pads worn by Bobby Holik of the New Jersey Devils during the Devils' 2000 Cup win; Mike Modano's helmet, worn during the Dallas Stars' 1999 Cup victory; shoulder pads worn by Pittsburgh's Ron Francis during the 1990s; Marcel Dionne's LA Kings gloves, worn during the mid-1980s; LA Kings socks worn by Glen Murray during the 1998–99 season; Cam Neely's skates, worn during his final season of play, 1995–96; and the stick Steve Yzerman used to record his 600th NHL goal.

SHER-WOOD PAT

LIPPMAN'S TOOL SHOP
DETROIT, MICHIGAN

NOR

LAFLEUR LOUISVILLE

FABRIQUE
AU CANADA

Terrific Twigs

Some of hockey's most remarkable goals and milestones, like Wayne Gretzky's 92nd single-season goal or Paul Henderson's Summit Series–winning goal, were registered with these sticks. To read more about each stick, see page 212.

NORTH

QUADRA GLASS 5000

CCM CU

EASTON

C.C.M. PATTERN MA

CCM

TITAN TP

B-WOOD PMF

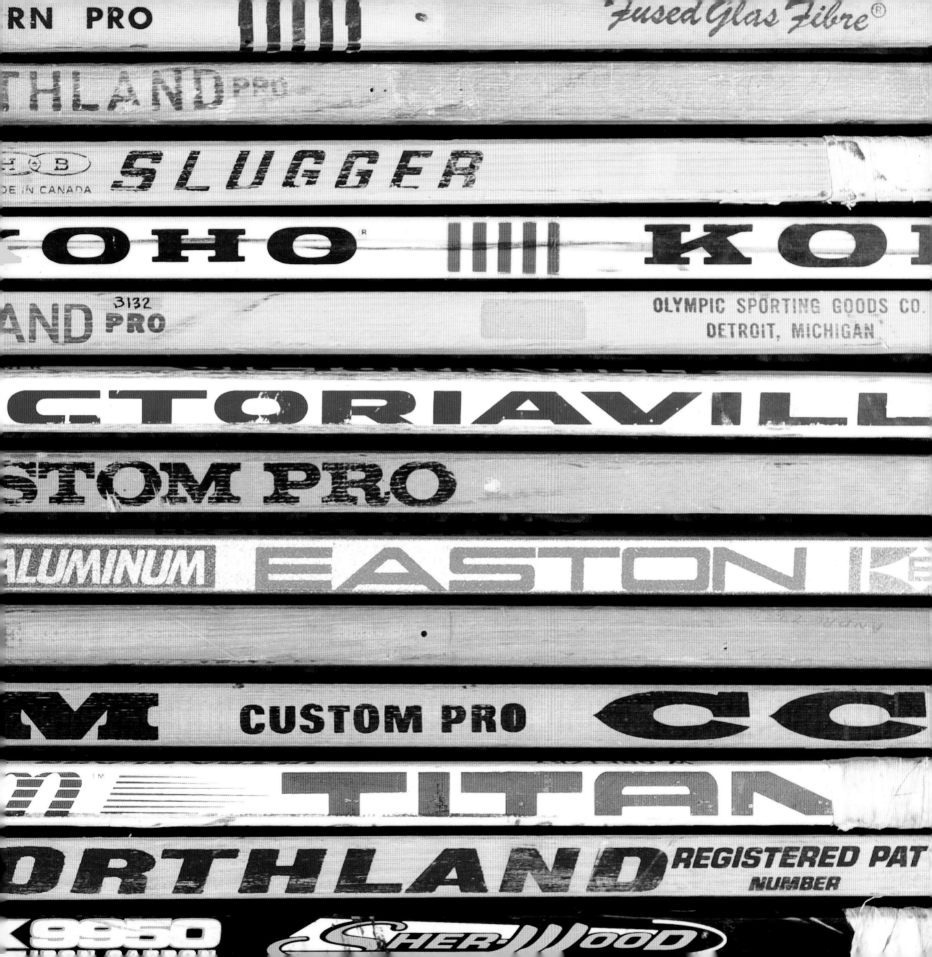

Weapon of Choice

Sticks used in professional, international and amateur women's play. To read more about each stick, see page 212.

SHER-WOOD

C·C·M· PRO CUSTOM PATTERN MADE PRO

SUPREME ONE95

SHER-WOOD

SHER-WOOD Feather-Lite 50 MADE IN CANADA

LOUISVILLE TPS

CLASSIC SILVER TIP EASTON

STOM C·C·M· PRO PATTERN MADE PRO

EASTON

NORTHLAND

TPS

CANADIEN CANADIEN 600

CHRISTIAN

ADIEN MID STIFF FLEX 01

Legendary Lumber

From landmark goals to milestone point totals, presented here are
sticks used by legends, as well as sticks used to create legends. To read
more about each stick, see page 213.

TPM 2020

The Last Goal He Ever Scored

The photographs above and at left show Bill Barilko as he sails through the air, watching what would be his overtime Stanley Cup–wining goal sail past Montreal's Gerry McNeil on April 21, 1951. The goal was Barilko's last, as he and Dr. Henry Hudson, a friend, died tragically in a plane crash on their way to a fishing trip four months after this goal. The bodies of Barilko and Hudson were found 11 years later, in 1962, the same year the Leafs would next win the Cup.

Firsts and Lasts
Toronto's Bill Barilko used this puck to score his last NHL goal, an overtime Stanley Cup winner on April 21, 1951. To read more about Barilko, see pages 122–123. To the right are more pucks that represent professional hockey firsts and lasts. To read more about each puck, see page 214.

The Ultimate Competitor

Maurice "Rocket" Richard backhands a puck past Leafs netminder Harry Lumley during the 1953–54 season. The Rocket's trademark intensity earned him a reputation as a fierce competitor. The legend of his piercing eyes and steely resolve can be witnessed in this image, as his focus is undeterred despite the hook near his face from Harry Watson. Richard retired with 544 goals, the most in NHL history at the time, and he was the first player to ever score 500 career goals. The puck he scored his groundbreaking 500th goal with can be seen at right, in the center. To read more about each puck, see page 214.

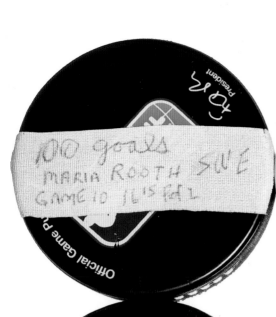

100 goals
MARIA ROOTH SWE
GAME 10 16½ Fd L

Official Game P...

President

OLYMPIC WINTER GAMES SALT LAKE 2002

QUEEN'S
Golden
Gaels

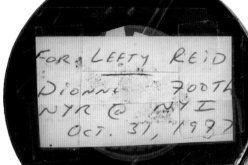

FOR LEFTY REID
DIONNE 700TH
NYR @ NYI
OCT. 31, 1987

PHOENIX
roadrunners

#622
DON PARSONS
ASST BY
JEFF PETRUIC
JAMI YODER

Mike ...land
Rec. ...48

BINGHAMTON
WHALERS

SVENSKA ISHOCKEY FORBUNDET
GODKÄND MATCHPUCK

The Golden Goal

A fan photo donated to the Hockey Hall of Fame shows a bird's-eye view of Sidney Crosby's "golden goal," scored 7:40 into overtime of the men's gold-medal final at the 2010 Vancouver Olympics. Canada defeated the U.S. 3–2, claiming Olympic gold for the second time since 2002. The game was the most-viewed hockey game in history, and Crosby's marker gave Team Canada the most gold medals by any nation in one Winter Olympic Games. To the right is the puck that Crosby slid through Ryan Miller's legs, which can be seen in the back of the net on this photo.

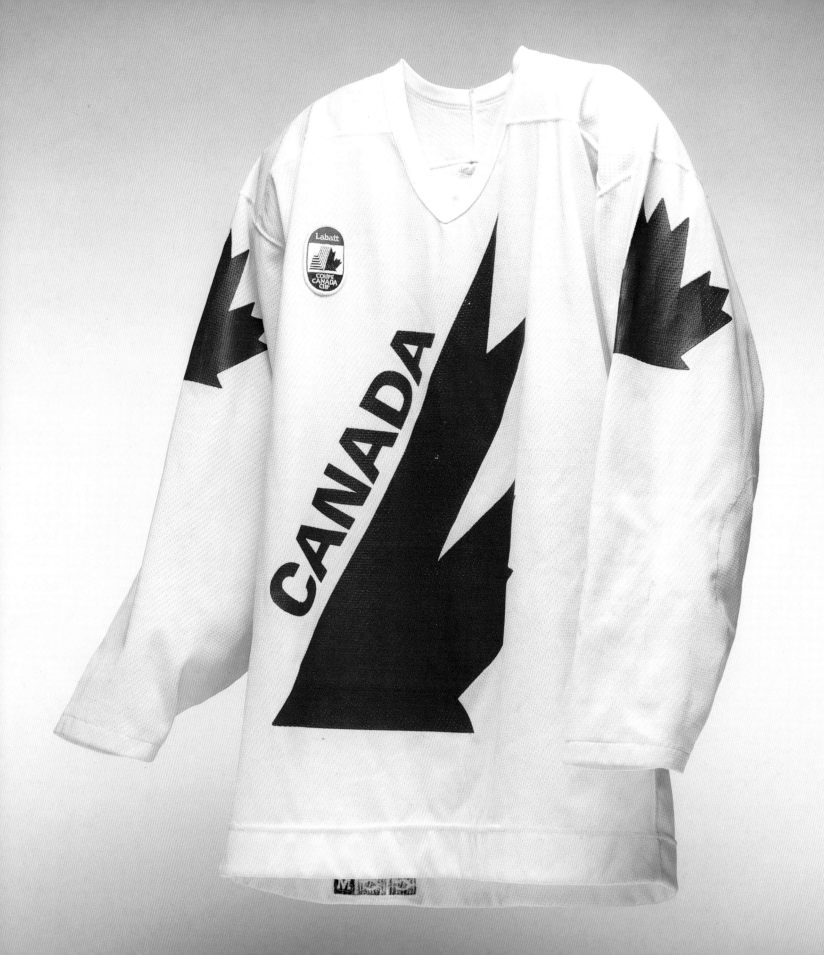

Magnificent Mario

Photographs in succession of Mario Lemieux streaking in on Russian goalie Sergei Mylnikov to score the championship-winning goal in a three-game final at the 1987 Canada Cup. The goal was scored with 1:26 left in regulation and was Lemieux's 11th goal in nine games. With that goal, the Canadians came back from a 3–0 deficit to win the game 6–5. The Team Canada jersey, whose logo is modeled after the Canada Cup, worn by Mario Lemieux to score the tournament-winning goal can be seen at left.

Winnipeg Falcons Team Canada sweater worn by Konrad Johannesson at the 1920 Summer Olympics in Antwerp, Belgium, which was the first Olympics to feature hockey. Canada won gold.

Pink Team Canada jersey worn by Sue Sherer during the 1990 Women's World Championship, the first women's tournament sanctioned by the IIHF. Canada won gold.

Trail Smoke Eaters sweater worn by Benny Hayes while representing Canada at the 1939 World Championship. The Smoke Eaters went undefeated to win the gold medal.

Team Canada 72 Summit Series jersey worn by defenseman Rod Seiling.

Jersey worn by Viacheslav Fetisov during the 1988 Calgary Olympics. Fetisov tied for a tournament-best nine assists to help the USSR claim the gold.

Sweater worn by Vladislav Tretiak during the 1973 World Championship in Moscow. The Soviets went undefeated to win the tournament on home ice.

Home-ice Advantage

Team USA jerseys worn by father-and-son hockey stars Bill and Dave Christian while representing their country at the 1960 Olympics in Squaw Valley, California, and the 1980 Olympics in Lake Placid, New York, respectively. The sweater in the foreground was worn by Bill Christian throughout the Squaw Valley Olympics. The host Americans went undefeated in seven games and captured the country's first Olympic gold medal in hockey, with Bill finishing second in team scoring, with 13 points. The jersey in the background was worn by Dave Christian during the Lake Placid Olympics, including the famed "Miracle on Ice" 4–3 victory over the Soviets. The host Americans stunned the hockey world when they captured the United States' second Olympic gold medal. Above is a picture of the 1960 team celebrating their gold-medal victory.

Spinorama!

Jerseys from the IHL, ECHL and WHA get put through the spin cycle.

▲ *Top row, left to right*: Goalie Mike Ralph's 1975–76 Port Huron Flags jersey; Fort Wayne Komets jersey worn by Len Thornson for his final season of pro hockey, 1968–69. Thornson finished as the IHL's all-time points leader (1,252). *Bottom row, left to right*: Kevin Knopp's Lexington Men O' War jersey worn for the franchise's inaugural ECHL game, on October 11, 2002; Saginaw Gears jersey, circa 1970s. Saginaw won two Turner Cups (1977, 1981).

► *Top row, left to right*: Paul Hoganson's 1975–76 Cincinnati Stingers jersey; WHA New England Whalers jersey worn by Jack Carlson before he joined the NHL's Minnesota North Stars in 1979; Minnesota Fighting Saints jersey worn by Dave Hanson for the 1976–77 WHA season. Hanson became famous that year for portraying one of the Hanson brothers in the movie *Slap Shot*. *Bottom row, left to right*: Darryl Maggs' 1975–76 WHA Denver Spurs jersey (Denver moved to Ottawa and became the Civics on January 2, 1976); Toronto Toros jersey worn by Wayne Dillon, who scored 160 points in two seasons with Toronto, 1973–75.

◄ Former NHL goaltender Ed Chadwick wore this California Golden Seals jacket while scouting talent for the Oakland-based club in 1970–71.

► Leather jacket worn by Howie Morenz after Chicago acquired him from Montreal, prior to the 1934–35 NHL season.

◄ Leather jacket worn by Sudbury Wolves manager Harry Towns while leading the Wolves to a gold medal at the 1938 World Championship in Czechoslovakia.

► Jacket that belonged to Vancouver's Roger Neilson while he coached the Campbell Conference at the 1983 NHL All-Star Game, a 9-3 victory for Neilson's team.

◄ Cardigan worn by 12-year Toronto Maple Leafs veteran Bob Davidson, who also served as captain from 1943 to 1945.

◄ Providence Reds jersey worn by Don McKenney for the 1969–70 AHL season, his final season of pro hockey.

► Cleveland Falcons sweater worn by defenseman Joe Bretto for the 1936–37 International-American Hockey League season. The IAHL changed its name to AHL in 1940.

◄ AHL All-Star jersey worn by Frank Mathers during one of the six All-Star Games he participated in during the 1950s.

► Raffi Torres wore this Hamilton Bulldogs jersey during the 2003 AHL playoffs, including the Calder Cup final, a seven game loss to the Houston Aeros.

Gord Didier's St. Catharines Tee Pees training camp jersey from the 1959–60 Ontario Hockey Association season.

Bobby Clarke's jersey from the 1968–69 Flin Flon Bombers of the Western Canadian Junior Hockey League. Clarke's Bombers won the WCJHL Championship.

Lethbridge Broncos jersey worn by Ron Sutter for the 1982–83 Western Hockey League season.

Gordon "Red" Berenson's University of Michigan Wolverines sweater from the 1960–61 NCAA season.

Hamilton Fincups jersey worn by Danny Shearer for the 1975–76 Ontario Major Junior A Hockey season.

Clarkson University Golden Knights jersey worn by All-American Craig Conroy for his senior season, in 1993–94.

Hilda Ranscombe's Preston Rivulettes sweater from the 1930s. The Rivulettes were Canadian champs for the entire decade, losing only 2 of 350 games.

Montreal Canadiens sweater worn by superstar and fan favorite Howie Morenz during the 1930s.

Cecil Blachford's Montreal Wanderers sweater from the 1909 ECHA season. Blachford did not play but won the Stanley Cup with the club in 1906, '07 and '08.

New York Americans sweater worn by Harvey "Busher" Jackson between 1939 and 1941.

Sweater worn by the Chicago Black Hawks' Doug Bentley throughout the 1947–48 NHL season.

Boston Bruins sweater worn by Milt Schmidt during his first stint with the club, from 1936 to 1942.

► Commemorative 25th anniversary sweater worn by Bruins forward Woody Dumart during the 1948–49 NHL season.

Ron Francis' 1986–87 Hartford Whalers jersey.

Chicago jersey worn by Jonathan Toews during home games of the 2010 Stanley Cup final.

Quebec Nordiques jersey worn by Michel Goulet between 1980 and 1984.

Calgary Flames jersey worn by Sergei Priakin, the first Soviet to be given permission to play in the NHL, during the 1988–89 season.

Brett Hull's jersey from his first full season with St. Louis, 1988–89.

◄ Jerseys from Wayne Gretzky's first year in the NHL, 1979–80, with the Edmonton Oilers, and his first season with the LA Kings, 1988–89.

Gearing Up

Gear from various NHL players spanning multiple eras, styles of play and technological advancements. To read more about the gear in each stall, see pages 215–216.

HONORING

3

THE GAME

Hockey has long been a sport that honors its best. Amateur teams in Canada have been playing for ornate cups, bowls and custom-crafted trophies, like the World Senior Championship Trophy and the O'Brien Cup, since the late 1800s. But it was Lord Stanley's Dominion Hockey Challenge Cup, and its "challenge" rules, that gave early elite-level hockey a true prize. First awarded in the winter of 1893 to the Montreal Amateur Athletic Association hockey club, Lord Stanley's cup has been awarded every year since then – with the exception of the 1918–19 championship (canceled due to Spanish influenza) and the 2004–05 NHL lockout season – for the past 113 years. The long-standing tradition of the best North American hockey club being awarded the Stanley Cup, now contested once a year among clubs from the NHL, makes the Stanley Cup the oldest still-contested trophy in North American professional sports.

But the Stanley Cup is only one of hockey's splendid prizes. The following pages display famous, interesting and unique awards, honors and tributes from professional, international and amateur play. Some are new and many are old; some are for individual exploits and many more are for championship-winning teams. All together, they create a snapshot of one of hockey's most enduring legacies: giving awards.

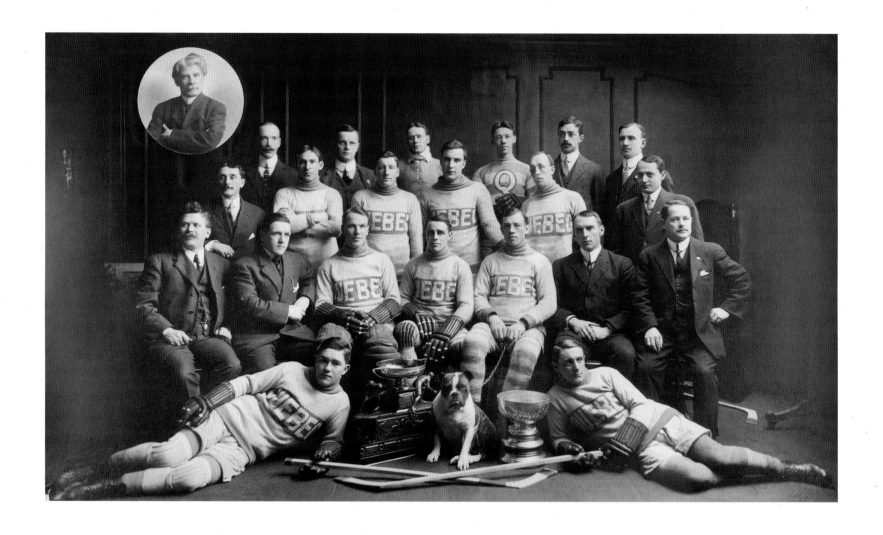

Old-time Hockey

The Quebec Bulldogs, National Hockey Association champions for the 1911–12 and 1912–13 seasons, are shown in this team picture with both the O'Brien Trophy (awarded to the NHA champion) and the Stanley Cup, which the Bulldogs won in 1912 and 1913. The O'Brien Trophy, seen at right, has a long history in professional hockey. In 1910 Senator J. O'Brien, in recognition of his son J. Ambrose O'Brien's large roll in helping to organize the NHA, donated the trophy to the league so it could be used as its championship prize. After the demise of the NHA in 1917, the trophy was awarded to the league champions of the NHL, but it was replaced in this role by the Prince of Wales Trophy. The trophy was retired, but then it was repurposed in 1939 and was awarded annually to the losing Stanley Cup finalist. The O'Brien Trophy was officially retired by the NHL at the end of the 1949–50 season, the New York Rangers being the last team to claim it.

Historic Hardware

Trophies, cups and bowls from hockey's formative years and from some of
hockey's once important and now defunct leagues. To read about the trophies
above and to the left, see pages 216–217.

Medals of Distinction

A selection of medals awarded to both teams and individuals. To read more about who earned these medals, see page 217.

The Calder Cup, awarded to the champions of the American Hockey League, is the most prestigious minor-professional trophy in hockey. The Calder Cup has been awarded annually since 1936.

The 2009 Hockey Hall of Fame induction class brandishes their induction rings. *From left to right*: Brett Hull, Lou Lamoriello, Brian Leetch, Luc Robitaille and Steve Yzerman. On the right are various Stanley Cup rings. *From front to back, left to right*: the first-ever Stanley Cup ring, awarded to the Montreal Amateur Athletic Association's Billy Barlow in 1893; Bill Hay's 1961 championship ring; Calgary owner D.K. Seaman's 1989 championship ring; a Detroit 2008 championship ring specially issued to the Hockey Hall of Fame; a Pittsburgh Penguins 2009 championship ring inscribed to the Hockey Hall of Fame; specially issued ring from Anaheim's 2007 championship that is inscribed to the Hockey Hall of Fame; Coach Bob Johnson's 1991 Pittsburgh Penguins championship ring; duplicate of Chicago Blackhawks' Jonathan Toews' 2010 championship ring, which was specially issued to the Hockey Hall of Fame.

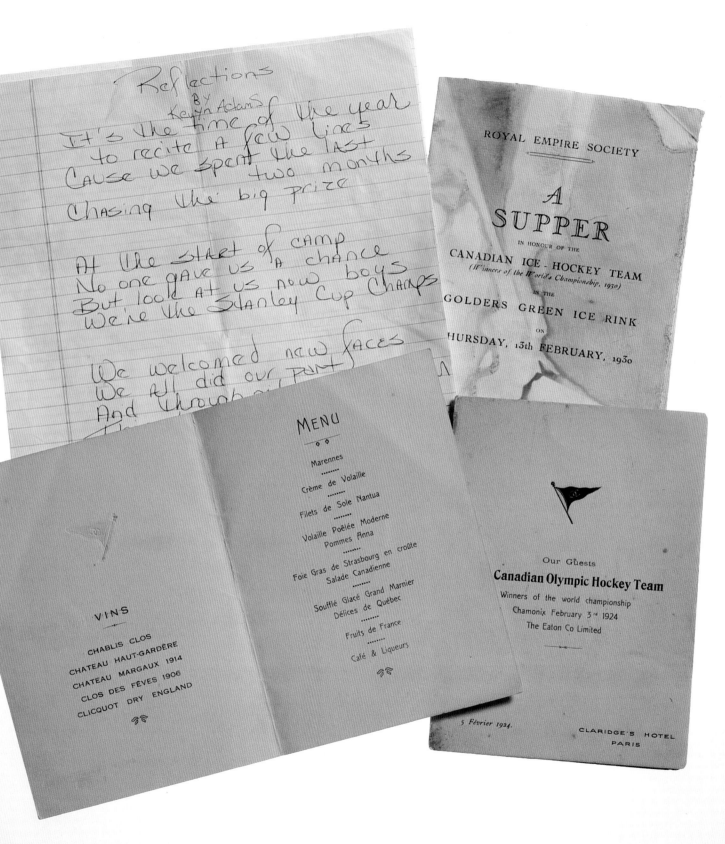

Reflections
By
Kevin Adams

It's the time of the year
to recite a few lines
Cause we spent the last
two months
Chasing the big prize

At the start of camp
No one gave us a chance
But look at us now boys
We're the Stanley Cup Champs

We welcomed new faces
We all did our part
And throughout

ROYAL EMPIRE SOCIETY

A
SUPPER
IN HONOUR OF THE
CANADIAN ICE-HOCKEY TEAM
(Winners of the World's Championship, 1930)
IN THE
GOLDERS GREEN ICE RINK
ON
THURSDAY, 13th FEBRUARY, 1930

MENU
o o
Marennes
········
Crème de Volaille
········
Filets de Sole Nantua
········
Volaille Poêlée Moderne
Pommes Anna
········
Foie Gras de Strasbourg en croûte
Salade Canadienne
········
Soufflé Glacé Grand Marnier
Délices de Québec
········
Fruits de France
········
Café & Liqueurs
ૐ

VINS

CHABLIS CLOS
CHATEAU HAUT-GARDÈRE
CHATEAU MARGAUX 1914
CLOS DES FEVES 1906
CLICQUOT DRY ENGLAND
ૐ

Our Guests
Canadian Olympic Hockey Team
Winners of the world championship
Chamonix February 3rd 1924
The Eaton Co Limited

5 Février 1924.

CLARIDGE'S HOTEL
PARIS

Men of Influence

▲ A selection of Tommy Ivan's personal trophies from his days coaching the Detroit Red Wings and managing the Chicago Black Hawks rests on the mantel in the Hockey Hall of Fame's Founders' Room. Jack Adams' pen set – awarded to him and his wife by the Michigan Federation of Race Tracks for his support of Michigan sporting life at the Jack Adams Testimonial Dinner on October 8, 1962 – sits on the desk along with the briefcase of Father David Bauer, the architect of the Canadian National Team program.

Dinner and Entertainment

◄ A celebratory poem written by Kevyn Adams of the Carolina Hurricanes, which was recited to his team after their 2005–06 Stanley Cup championship. To the right of the poem is the menu from a dinner given in honor of the 1930 World Championship winner, Team Canada. Underneath is the menu from a dinner honoring the 1924 Olympic gold-medal-winning Canadian team (interior and exterior of the menu are shown).

The front side of the Clarkson Cup, featuring the Inuit goddess Sedna. The masks on the stem and the provincial flowers around the base are also visible.

THE BIRTH OF THE CLARKSON CUP

| ADRIENNE CLARKSON

In the winter of 2004–05, during the National Hockey League lockout, it became clear to fans everywhere that the Stanley Cup would not be awarded that season. While talking with friends, I commented that it was a shame that women couldn't win the Stanley Cup if the men were not going to play. Somehow this got picked up by the newspapers and made a few headlines across Canada.

I had watched women's hockey for some time and had seen how good the competition was in the Olympics. I also knew that more and more young girls were playing hockey competitively. When I was growing up, there was no question that your skates, if you were a girl, would have to be figure skates. I have very weak ankles, and I could tell that my brother's skates were sturdier and would probably suit my feet better, which even then were flat. However, there was no question that I would wear figure skates, as they were more "feminine." Nobody took the idea of girls playing competitive hockey seriously.

For years women had been struggling to put together women's hockey leagues, to get practice time and to raise what were, compared to what even semi-professional men's leagues were able to raise, tiny amounts of money.

When the lockout in the NHL made everyone focus on the game, somehow those old longings I had for wearing hockey skates and the subconscious jealousy I must have felt looking at boys playing hockey all came together. It seemed the perfect time to create a new cup for women's hockey and to give some much-needed recognition to women's hockey competitions. Two previous governor generals had established the most

durable sports awards in Canada: Lord Grey had created the cup for Canadian football and Lord Stanley the one for men's hockey. Both cups have been awarded for over 100 years.

It was initially difficult to get the idea of a new trophy for women's hockey accepted, but I was impressed right from my first meetings with hockey executives Brenda Andress and Fran Ryder, who were totally committed and believed that establishing the Clarkson Cup, as it came to be called, would be a good thing for the game.

I had meetings with Bob Nicholson of Hockey Canada through 2004 and 2005. Progress seemed slow, but I was heartened by the fact that even the Stanley Cup had gotten off to a slow start. Lord Stanley had already vacated his position as governor general when his cup was finally presented for the first time, in 1893.

It seemed to me that the best thing to do to get things moving was to have the physical cup created so people could see for themselves what was at stake. I commissioned the design for the cup from several artists that I had met at the Nunavut Arctic College's silver program. I wanted the Clarkson Cup to stand as a symbol of female strength, endurance and the ability to triumph against all odds.

The design features the Inuit goddess Sedna across one side. Sedna is the perfect symbol of endurance. According to the Inuit legend, she had a very hard life. She was unhappily married to a man who turned out to be an evil bird, and her father rescued her. However, as he was taking her away in his kayak, a terrible storm came up. Terrified that they would both drown if the overloaded kayak capsized, he chose to save himself and threw Sedna overboard. Showing her perseverance, Sedna refused to let go of the kayak. In desperation, her father cut off her fingers one by one. As each of her fingers fell into the water, a different sea creature was created – the seal, the fish, the walrus and the whale. As a result, Sedna controls all of the animals of the sea, and her spirit rests on the ocean floor. She is portrayed in Inuit art as having the head and torso of a woman and the tail of a fish.

To me, this symbol of female courage and final triumph over adversity was perfect for the Clarkson Cup. There are also many other images on the cup. The beautiful and powerful Sedna is holding a hockey stick and puck in her hands. On the cup's handles are images of the sea creatures created from Sedna's fingers, which look as though they are swimming upward from the stem of the trophy toward the top in an attempt to reach the surface. There are maple leaves on the top of each handle, and at the bottom of the cup is a ring of provincial and territorial flowers to honor Canada. The stem of the cup is covered with ancient masks that resemble hockey masks and the multiple faces of the Inuit. The overall effect is that of a throng cheering their team to victory.

On the back of the cup is my crest from the office of the governor general. Like the front, the back of the cup also features many symbols. A Chinese-style phoenix rising from the flames represents my family's roots and is also a symbol of rebirth and re-creation. There is a maple leaf that indicates my family's new beginnings as Canadians, an image of the Royal Crown, which symbolizes the office of governor general, and a loon that symbolizes the magnificent beauty of the North. The tiger is my favorite animal, since I was born in the Year of the Tiger, according to the ancient Chinese astrological calendar. On a scroll at the base of the design is the phrase *Verum solum dicatur, verum solum accipiatur.* This is derived from a prayer, "May only the truth be spoken, may only the truth be heard." A favorite phrase of mine, I believe it is what we should all expect to receive and hear: truth and integrity.

After the cup was created and people could see it, things moved a little faster. The Clarkson Cup was presented as a challenge cup for the first time in 2009, after a championship game held in Kingston, Ontario, between the Montreal Stars of the Canadian Women's Hockey League and the Minnesota Whitecaps of the Western Women's Hockey League, with Montreal winning 3–1. As I made the first ever championship presentation of the Clarkson Cup, I was thrilled that it represented the fulfillment of so many people's dreams.

My dream is that the Clarkson Cup will become a part of every young girl's dream to play in, or even just watch, a professional women's hockey league.

There are still organizational problems in determining how the Clarkson Cup will be incorporated into women's professional hockey, but this is inevitable when anything new is starting up. Women's hockey must now become a truly professional sport with funding that will allow the best players to devote themselves totally to the game, without having to maintain day jobs. This could very well happen under the wing of the NHL and would certainly add a spectacular dimension to the game that all of us love and so many women play so well.

I knew that the Clarkson Cup had achieved all that I had hoped when Cassie Campbell, the former Olympic team captain, said that the Clarkson Cup, "gives women's hockey the legitimacy it deserves."

THE RIGHT HONOURABLE ADRIENNE CLARKSON, long-time journalist and best-selling author, is the 26th Governor General of Canada. Her name and crest adorns the Clarkson Cup, given to the champion of North American women's professional hockey.

The backside of the Clarkson Cup,
featuring the intricate crest of the
Right Honourable Adrienne Clarkson.

JUNIOR CANADIAN CHAMPIONSHIP.
O. H. A.
MEMORIAL CHALLENGE CUP

In Remembrance

The Memorial Cup, which was created to honor those who lost their lives in World War I. To read more about the Memorial Cup, see page 218.

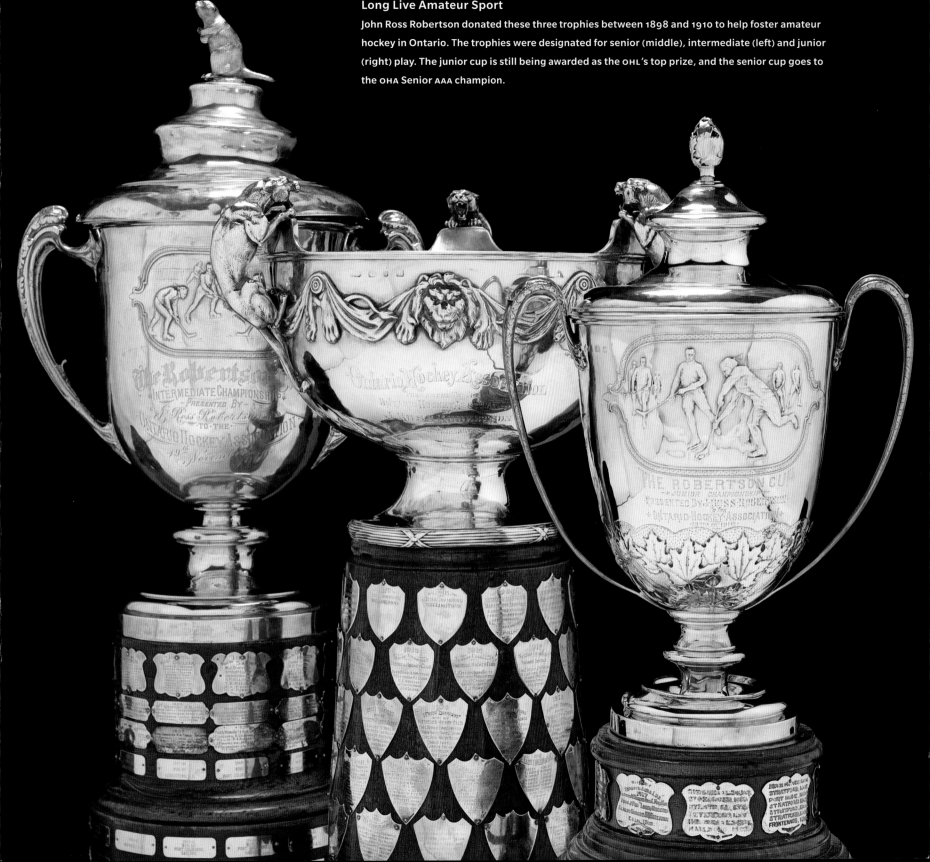

Long Live Amateur Sport

John Ross Robertson donated these three trophies between 1898 and 1910 to help foster amateur hockey in Ontario. The trophies were designated for senior (middle), intermediate (left) and junior (right) play. The junior cup is still being awarded as the OHL's top prize, and the senior cup goes to the OHA Senior AAA champion.

Pro Challenge

Team USA poses with the 1996 World Cup, which they earned after defeating Canada 5–2 in Game 3 in the best-of-three final. On the facing page at the far right is the World Cup awarded in 1996, used solely for that tournament, as well as three other pro challenge trophies. In the foreground is the Canada Cup, the forerunner to the World Cup and the preeminent professional challenge tournament between 1976 and 1991. To the left is the World Cup awarded in 2004, which was designed by Canadian architect Frank Gehry. It was meant to symbolize ice and steel, but its unconventional design made the trophy the focus of much ridicule. It replaced the 1996 World Cup and was also awarded only once, in 2004. Team Canada scooped the trophy that year, the last World Cup to be played to date. At the top sits the NHL Challenge Cup, awarded to the Soviet National Team after they defeated NHL All-Stars in a best-of-three series in 1979.

WORLD JUNIOR CHAMPIONSHIP

INTERNATIONAL ICE HOCKEY FEDERATION

WINNER

World Junior Championship plate that was awarded to
Team Canada at the 1985 tournament.

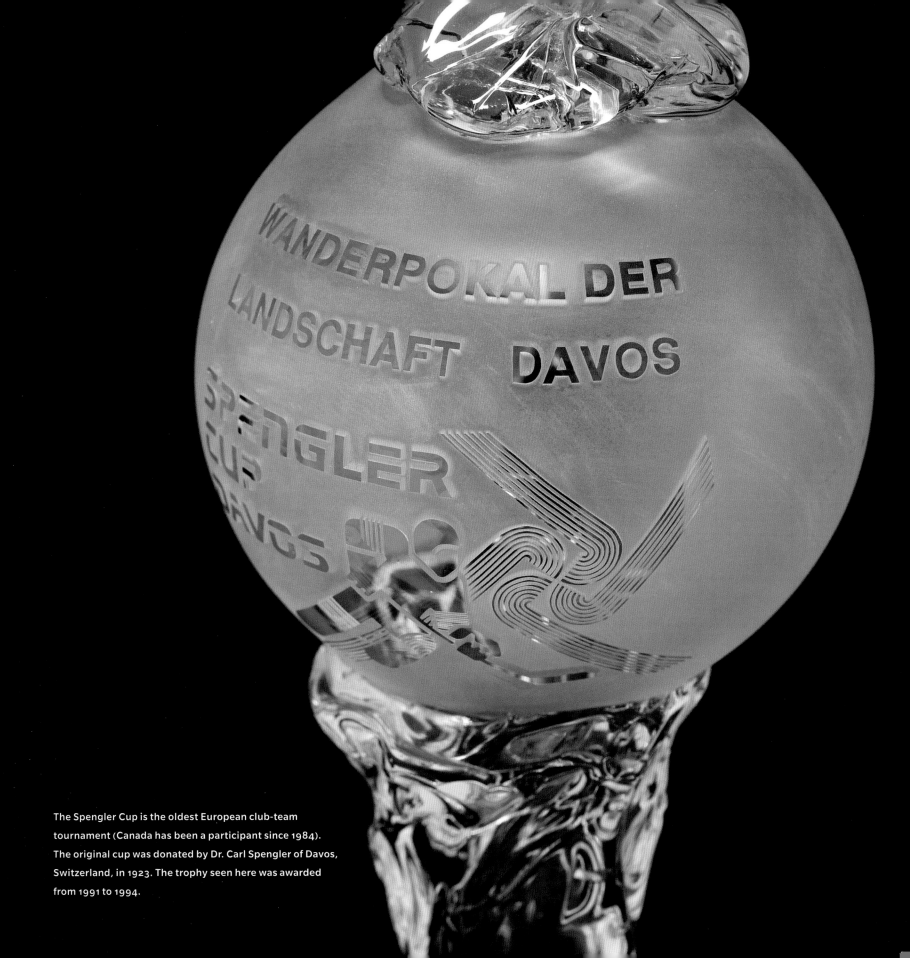

The Spengler Cup is the oldest European club-team
tournament (Canada has been a participant since 1984).
The original cup was donated by Dr. Carl Spengler of Davos,
Switzerland, in 1923. The trophy seen here was awarded
from 1991 to 1994.

Walking with the Great One
A plaster cast of Wayne Gretzky's feet that was originally used by Daoust to mold Gretzky's hockey skates. The mold was mounted, painted gold and given to Wayne's father, Walter, as a unique gift after Wayne scored his 50th goal in his 39th game, shattering the record of 50 goals in 50 games shared by Maurice Richard and Mike Bossy.

Clockwise from top left: The Coupe Purolator trophy; the Upper Deck NHL All-Rookie Team Trophy; Budweiser NHL Man of the Year Trophy; Shipstads and Johnson Perpetual Challenge Trophy.

To read more about these four trophies, see page 218.

The NHL Collection
Some of the many cups and trophies awarded by the NHL. See pages 219–220
for more information on the histories of these awards.

Dominion Hockey Challenge Cup
Lord Stanley's original cup, donated in 1892 and now on permanent display in the bank vault at the Hockey Hall of Fame. To the left is the Presentation Stanley Cup. This is the cup that makes its way to center ice every year to be presented to the NHL's best.

RECORDING

THE GAME

Storytellers are society's record-keepers. A good storyteller can turn the actions of ordinary men into the exploits of heroes, can build legends, can create villains and can make the impossible seem possible. In hockey, it was storytellers who let the world know of the unmatched skill of "Cyclone" Taylor, the fiery zeal of "Rocket" Richard and the awesome talent of the young Wayne Gretzky. They bellowed the out-of-town game results to theater audiences in the early 1900s as the reports came in over the telegraph wire, and they joined us in our living rooms over the airwaves while doing live play-by-play.

But storytelling is more than just game reports, word of mouth and hype. The statistician, the minute-taker, the beat reporter, the scrapbooker, the archivist, the sportscaster, the film crew and the schedule-maker – all create a physical record of the game. Their efforts have created hockey's record, and like most sports this record is full of tales of triumph and defeat, winners and losers, stars and scoundrels.

Presented in the following pages are portraits of hockey's record, a selection of some of the ways that hockey's story has been told and ways in which it has been preserved for future storytellers.

▲ Foster Hewitt, radio pioneer, was the eyes and ears of generations of hockey fans across Canada and the United States. To the delight of radio listeners, Hewitt called thousands of hockey games, including national, World and Olympic championships in Canada, the United States and Europe. In this image, Hewitt is in his familiar position in the radio gondola above the action at Maple Leaf Gardens. Today hockey broadcasters aspire to win a Foster Hewitt Award, given annually by the NHL Broadcasters' Association to those who have made outstanding contributions to their profession and the game.

◄ Terry Sawchuk – caught in a moment of postgame reflection as he sits in a studio in full gear – waits to be interviewed on *Hockey Night in Canada*.

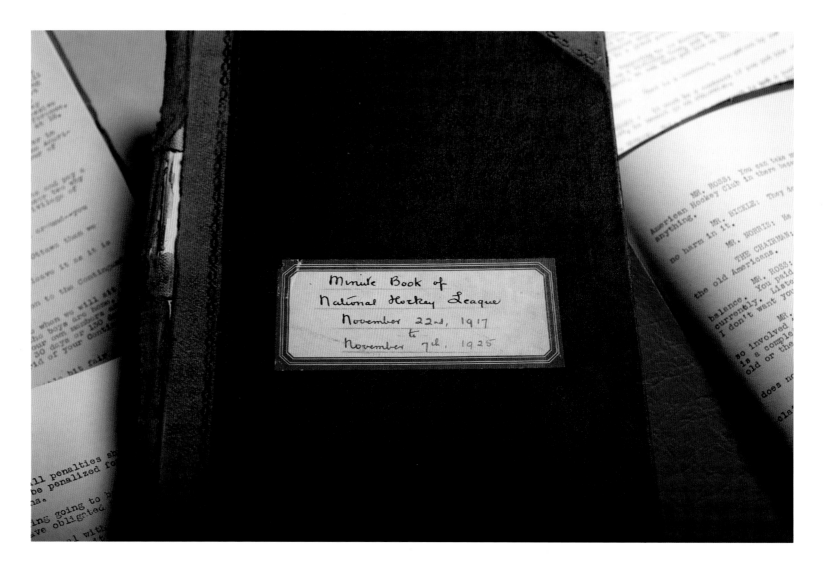

Put It in Writing

▲ The official minute book of the National Hockey League, started on November 22, 1917, four days prior to the now-famous meeting at the Windsor Hotel in Montreal, where the NHL board of governors founded the league. It was while attempting to avoid dissolving the National Hockey Association that the NHL came to be. On November 26, 1917, the new NHL board of governors adopted the 25-page constitution of the defunct National Hockey Association as the league's first governing document. On December 19, 1917, the NHL finally took to the ice.

▶ Various hockey contracts, including pre-NHL contracts for the services of Art Ross for the 1909–10 Haileybury Hockey Club, "Cyclone" Taylor for the 1909–10 Renfrew Hockey Club (signed on Windsor Hotel stationery) and Newsy Lalonde for the 1910–11 and 1912–13 Montreal Canadiens, as well as NHL contracts for Howie Meeker and Ted Kennedy and a minor pro contract for goalie Sal Messina.

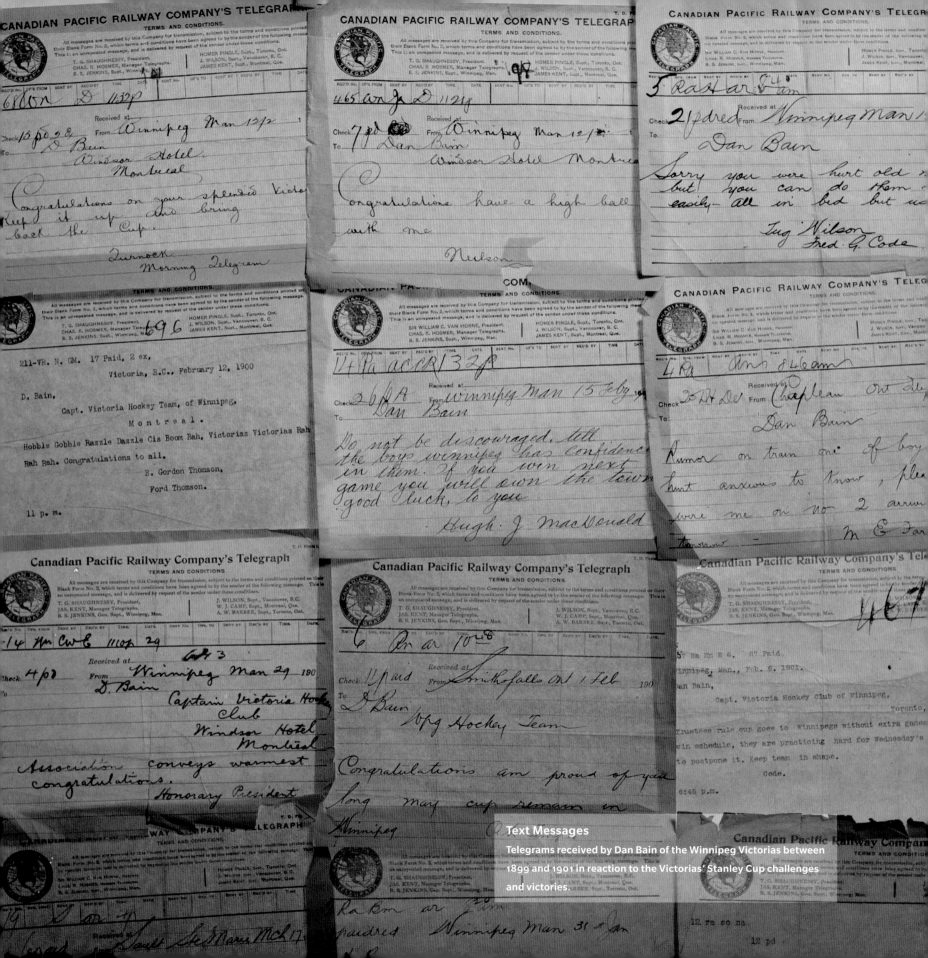

Cut and Paste

A small assortment of the hundreds of scrapbooks kept by enthusiasts and players that are now in the collection at the Hockey Hall of Fame.

Broadcasting Hockey
Iconic items from the halcyon days of hockey broadcasting, including:
the iconic CBC powder-blue blazer worn by *Hockey Night in Canada*
commentator Dick Irvin; the Sports Network blazer worn by *SportsDesk*
host Jim Van Horne; the "200 Club" helmet (created by the Philadelphia
Flyers when four Flyers each accumulated over 200 penalty minutes in
the same season) worn by Flyers broadcaster Gene Hart as a good luck
charm; and a 16-millimeter film camera used by Joe Black to film NHL
games in Toronto during the 1950s and 1960s.

REPORTING THE GAME

| **JAMES DUTHIE**

We were in a commercial break before overtime in the gold-medal hockey game at the 2010 Winter Olympics. American forward Zach Parise had just stunned Canada, the team – and the nation – with a dramatic tying goal in the dying seconds of the third period. As I sat with my CTV colleagues, Darren Pang, Nick Kypreos and Bob McKenzie, on our high-tech retractable TV studio perched above the Zamboni entrance, I turned and said, "Well boys, I'm thinking this is going to be the only time in our lives we'll do a hockey panel in front of 15 million people. Enjoy!"

Turns out I was a little low. It was 22 million. The most-watched television event in Canadian history. By a landslide.

Our seats were 30 feet from where Sidney Crosby's game-winner was fired. I wish I could tell you I had some profound epiphany at that moment about how far hockey, and media coverage of the game, had come since the game was first broadcast across the country in the 1930s. Frankly, I was just trying to make sure I didn't say anything stupid.

It was a man – a spunky 83-year-old wearing a Team Canada sweater and a gold medal around his neck – who sat a few sections away from me that day, who would give me a true appreciation of how much the way hockey is reported and recorded has changed.

His name is Gordie Robertson, and he was a member of the Edmonton Mercurys team that won hockey gold for Canada at the 1952 Olympics in Oslo, Norway, the last hockey gold Canada would win until Salt Lake City in 2002.

When Gordie had his golden moment in 1952, there were not 22 million people watching at home. There weren't 10,000 media representatives from around the world covering it. There weren't 27 cameras showing every possible angle of the goal. No super-slo-mo. No instant Tweets ("YES! Siiiiiiiiid!!!!!"). No countless camera-phone fan reactions posted within seconds on Facebook.

In fact, when the Mercurys won gold, no one in Canada knew, at least not for a while.

"I had to call [my family] when we got back to the Olympic Village," Gordie recalled with a laugh. "We had our celebration and got our medals, and then when we got back to the village, I asked if I could use the phone. They said, 'You're one of those Canadian hockey players who won the gold, of course you can use the phone!' So I called my Dad and Mom and my wife, who were all back at the house in Trail, BC. That's how they found out we'd won gold! A few weeks later some friends went to the movies, and they showed a little clip of us winning in one of those *News of the World* films they used to show before the movie ran. That was the first time anyone actually got to see part of the game!"

I'm not old enough to have stories like Gordie Robertson's, from the days of newsreels at the movies and Foster Hewitt on the radio. But during my 35-year love affair with the game, I've been able to go from waiting for the morning paper so I could read the box scores to having an up-to-the-minute app for my smartphone that gives me the details of every goal seconds after it is scored. Today, the moment a fantastic deke or a controversial hit happens, it is posted on YouTube, Tweeted hundreds of times and discussed instantly and endlessly by panels on TV and by fans on Internet chat sites. Every second of every game is everywhere.

An assortment of newspapers and magazines from Canada, the United States and Russia that cover hockey games, profile hockey personalities and report hockey news.

Take the NHL trade deadline. When I first started in broadcasting, in the early 1990s, the trade deadline was a tiny blip on the radar of the NHL season. On the day of the deadline, the trades came in on our wire service as the NHL announced them late in the afternoon. We'd rip the wire copy off and calmly report the deal on the 6 p.m. sportscast. Very few trades were actually "broken." They were just made and announced in due time.

Fast-forward 20 years, and the NHL trade deadline is big business. It started with TSN doing some regular updates, which then turned into a one-hour show, which then ballooned into *Tradecentre* – a 10-hour epic, featuring more than a dozen analysts in studio. And TSN is just one of several networks providing breathless all-day coverage of every deal.

The demand for professional sports coverage has never been greater. Fans – *fan*atics – are consumed by a need to marvel at their heroes and scorn their villains. Fandom has always been this way.

I fell in love with hockey as a 10-year-old boy. I'd spend hours wheeling around with my friend Sylvain Coderre on the suburban backyard rink his dad built. It had all the bells and whistles: boards, lights and grilled cheese on bagels waiting inside for us during our "intermissions."

On Saturday nights we'd watch the game. CBC would typically show the Toronto or Montreal game, but Chicago was my team and Tony Esposito and Cliff Koroll were my guys, so I looked forward to the intermissions more than the games. (Now that I host intermissions, I encourage all kids to do the same.) Sure, the games were good, but the intermissions had Peter Puck and, more importantly for me, "Showdown."

To a 10 year-old Canadian boy in the mid-70s, "Showdown" was *it*. For those who never saw it, or are too young to have seen it, the segment was broadcast between periods on *Hockey Night in Canada*. It was a skills competition between NHL stars, featuring 3-on-3 games, races and shootouts. And this was three decades before we saw shootouts every night in the NHL, so it was pure novelty and high drama. "Showdown" was all we talked about that week at school. It mattered more than the games: "Did you see

Darryl Sittler versus Rick MacLeish? That was awesome!" I found out much later that the whole series was filmed over a couple of days before the season started, but that didn't matter. At the time, "Showdown" was as important as which team won the Cup.

We were rabid about it then the way kids today are rabid about YouTube posts of wicked dekes and cool viral commercials featuring NHL stars (Ovechkin's floating head!). "Showdown" was our YouTube.

My own hockey career never went far (though I still maintain I dominated our own street hockey version of "Showdown"). Deep scars remain from the day a friend told me I skated like a penguin. That didn't bode well for my chances of going first overall in the draft.

Somewhere along the way, I started to think that if I couldn't play, I'd sure love to talk about the game for a living. I'd watch Dave Hodge on *Hockey Night in Canada* and think, "That guy might just have the best job in the world." (I asked Dave later. He concurred.) Imagine the concept of hockey host to a kid: "That guy watches hockey games and gets to interview the players after. And he gets paid for this? Where do I sign up?"

And the blazers! As a kid I didn't like dressing up much. I'd stuff the one jacket and tie I had deep in my closet so I wouldn't have to wear them to church on Sundays. The CBC *Hockey Night in Canada* powder-blue blazer was different. To me, it was almost as cool as my white Black Hawks sweater with Esposito's No. 35 on the back (still my favorite uniform in sports). The blue blazer meant you were part of the National Hockey League, even if you weren't playing in it. This, I knew, was my only ticket to the show.

So, I'd turn down the volume of my TV and do my own play-by-play. Or Sylvain and I would interview each other after our games on his rink.

I walked into my high school guidance counselor's office in grade 11 and said, "What do I need to take in university to be a sports broadcaster?" The journalism program at Carleton University, in Ottawa, Ontario, was one of the options that came up on her computer, and I was pretty much sold on the spot.

I got my first real job out of university at the CTV station in Ottawa in 1989, as a news reporter. This was before the sports networks like TSN and ESPN ruled, and there were very few jobs for a wannabe sports anchor. So I would file my news reports as quickly as possible, and then I'd loiter in the sports department and listen to the station's lead sportscaster, Brian Smith, tell great hockey story after great hockey story. He was a former NHLer and a legendary yarn-spinner.

Smitty and his colleague Bill Patterson taught me how to put a sportscast together. They'd bang out scripts on old typewriters, using carbon paper so everyone who needed a copy got one. They'd always tell me the same thing, "Don't just give scores, tell stories. And always remember the local teams matter most."

On August 1st, 1995, Smitty was shot in the head by a deranged man as he left the news station. He died the next day. I would do the sportscast that night, still the hardest show I've ever done, and will ever do.

I replaced Smitty full-time in the sports department – my dream job, achieved in the worst possible way. I left the station less than two years later and briefly returned to news. It never felt right to get my big break by losing a friend and mentor. That was the mid-90s, when our coverage of sports, and hockey in particular, was changing at hyper-speed.

I was hired by TSN in the middle of that media revolution. I still remember the day my boss asked me if I liked writing. They needed some columnists for a new website they were launching, tsn.ca. "Sports content on the Internet? That'll never work," I thought to myself. I thought the same thing when I heard you'd soon be able to watch games on your phone. "Who would want to do that?" Lots of people, apparently.

It's tempting to get nostalgic about hockey's simpler time, when there was still an aura of mystery to the game and its players. A time when every game wasn't on TV and Saturday nights really meant something.

My 11-year-old son rolls his eyes when I say things like that. And he's right. He lives, we live, in a magical time, when everything we ever wanted to know about hockey is right there in front of us, at our finger tips.

I don't really buy those who say the art of storytelling has been lost in this age of rapid-fire highlights and 140-character-or-less game reports. There are still great storytellers, in newspaper and on TV, who have been able to reach new audiences with new technologies. I used to get a new Stan Fischler hockey book every Christmas as a kid. Now I follow him on Twitter!

The HBO hockey series *24/7 Penguins/Capitals: Road to the NHL Winter Classic,* for example, was epic storytelling. Those cameras took us places I never dreamed we'd go when I started in this business. It made the game look like art. When the last episode ended, I turned to my boy and said, "That reminded me of why I fell in love with hockey."

But I still have a soft spot for the old-school storytellers, like Gordie Robertson, who won that gold for Canada in Oslo six decades ago. He leaves me with one last story.

"I was the fighter on the Mercurys, even though I wasn't a very good one. Well, in one game this Czech player was holding my stick. I kept saying, 'Drop it!' He wouldn't, so I dropped my gloves and belted him one. Well, that sure wasn't allowed in the Olympics. They had to have a meeting to decide if I would be disciplined. Can you imagine the disgrace if I got kicked out of the Olympic Games? But there wasn't much reporting on it back then. No TV, no replays, so they let it slide. You imagine if I did that today? It would be all over the computer and the TV … It would be everywhere!"

Yes, today he would have lived in infamy as "Gordie the Goon." He laughs when I tell him this, and he reminds me that, though we live in a wondrous media age, there were advantages to his having had his golden moment in a much simpler time.

JAMES DUTHIE is host of the *NHL on TSN* and is the author of two books: *They Day I (Almost) Killed Two Gretzky's* and *They Call Me Killer: Tales From Junior Hockey's Legendary Hall-of-Fame Coach.*

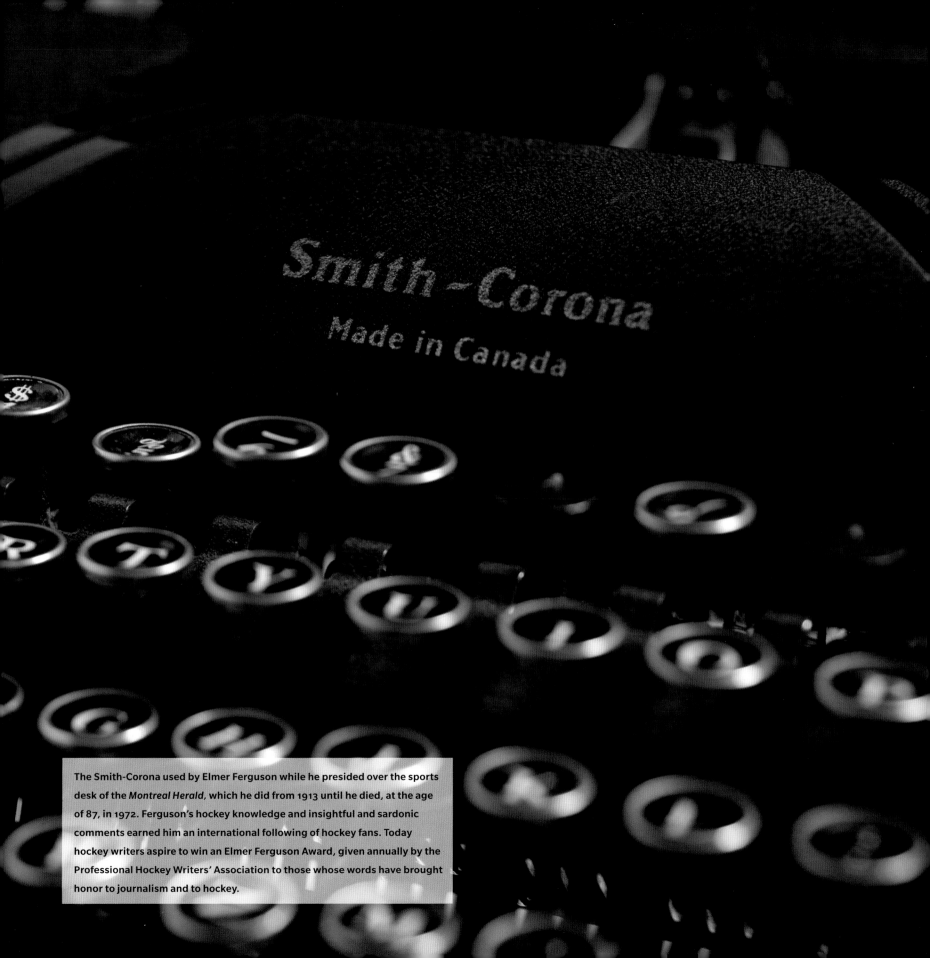

The Smith-Corona used by Elmer Ferguson while he presided over the sports desk of the *Montreal Herald*, which he did from 1913 until he died, at the age of 87, in 1972. Ferguson's hockey knowledge and insightful and sardonic comments earned him an international following of hockey fans. Today hockey writers aspire to win an Elmer Ferguson Award, given annually by the Professional Hockey Writers' Association to those whose words have brought honor to journalism and to hockey.

Spin the Black Circle

Hockey-themed records for hockey fans and music listeners, including game highlights, instructional recordings, team anthems, players in song and Al Melgard playing Chicago Stadium's legendary pipe organ.

Game Tape
Cans containing films depicting Stanley Cup finals, Howie Meeker giving
hockey instruction and player interviews – and much more – from the Hockey
Hall of Fame's vast film archive.

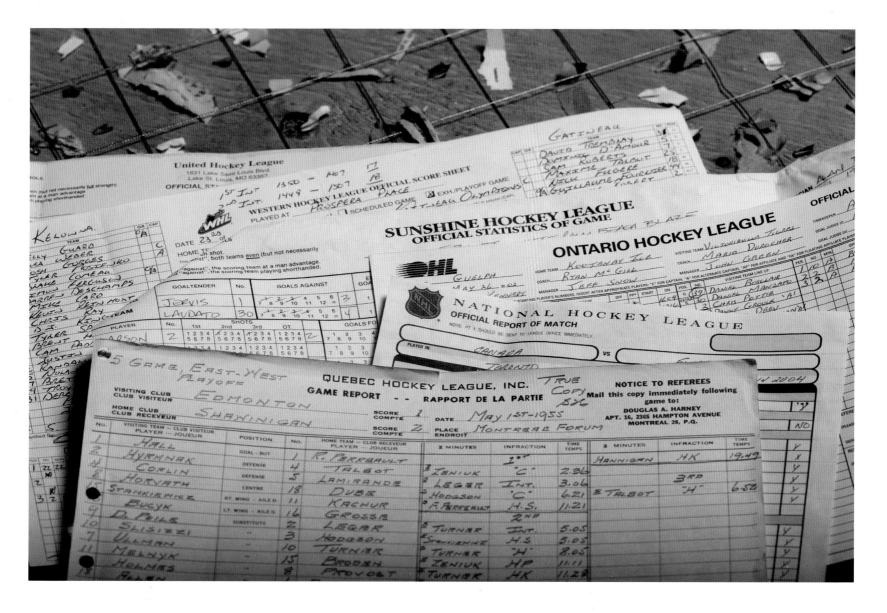

▲ Official game sheets are the physical and statistical record of every hockey game. Shown here
are meticulously kept game sheets from a variety of professional, minor pro and junior leagues.
The topmost sheet, from the 1955 Edinburgh Trophy challenge between the Western Hockey League's
Edmonton Flyers and the Quebec Hockey League's Shawinigan Falls, records that future Hall of
Famers Glenn Hall, Johnny Bucyk and Norm Ullman played for Edmonton, who lost the game, and
the series, despite their talented roster.

◄ Ticket stubs from various teams, leagues and marquee hockey events, including: Game 2 and Game 8 of the 1972
Summit Series; the final game of the 1979 NHL Challenge Cup; Game 1 of the 1996 World Cup of Hockey final; the gold-
medal game of the 1998 Olympics; the first annual Hockey Hall of Fame Game; the home opener of the Toronto Maple
Leafs' first complete season at the Air Canada Centre; a season's pass for the WHL's Edmonton Flyers; and a regular season
ticket from EHC Kloten of the Swiss A League.

98

Championship

Championnat de hockey sur
glace féminin de l'USIC

Feb. 26 to March 1
Concordia University

WESTERN · HOCKEY · LEAGUE

✝ SEATTLE
TOTEMS
VS
PORTLAND
BUCKAROOS
1965 · 1966

• VANCOUVER CANUCKS
• PORTLAND BUCKAROOS
• SAN FRANCISCO SEALS
• SEATTLE TOTEMS
• LOS ANGELES BLADES
• VICTORIA MAPLE LEAFS

Interlocking Schedule
American Hockey League

LIFORNIA
'72

ALS...
FOR FAMI
OF LATE
BELOVED CANADIEN
HOCKEY
STAR
★

TOUTES LES RECETTES
IRONT
A LA FAMILLE
TE JOUEUR

THE GREAT WINTER CARNIVAL OF 1889.
Montreal, 4th, 5th, 6th, 7th, 8th & 9th February.
Under the distinguished patronage of
Their Excellencies THE GOVERNOR GENERAL
and THE LADY STANLEY of Preston.

OFFICIAL PROGRAMME.

BOSTON GA
HOCK
AND INDOOR SPO
MAGAZIN

HOUSTON AEROS '73
OTTAWA

BASEL
Dolder ZÜRICH

COMETS

"Get Yer Program Here"
Programs from various hockey leagues, teams and eras,
including the program for Montreal's 1889 winter carnival,
which hosted "The Governor General and the Lady Stanley
of Preston." It was here that Lord Stanley witnessed his first
hockey game.

An assortment of pocket hockey schedules featuring team schedules, broadcast schedules, arena specific schedules and even train schedules.

Million-dollar Man

Frank Mahovlich backhands a puck against Chicago's Glenn Hall. The two All-Stars were nearly teammates when Tommy Ivan and James Norris of the Chicago Black Hawks met with Stafford Smythe and Harold Ballard of the Toronto Maple Leafs at the Royal York Hotel in Toronto the day before the 1961–62 All-Star Game. That evening Norris cut a $1 million check to the Leafs for the sale of Frank Mahovlich. The agreement to sell Mahovlich to Chicago was scrawled on a sheet of Royal York stationery and signed and witnessed by those in attendance. Toronto reneged on the deal the next morning, infuriating the Black Hawks and keeping Mahovlich a Leaf. The agreement and un-cashed check can be seen to the right.

AFTERWORD
Preserving Hockey History at the Hockey Hall of Fame

| **RISTO PAKARINEN**

Hockey history is full of important, inspiring capital *M* moments: the cups, the medals, the records and the milestones – the once-in-a-lifetime scenarios. The physical items immortalized in these moments are what first come to mind when you think of the Hockey Hall of Fame, items like the Stanley Cup, Sidney Crosby's Olympic gold medal–winning puck and stick, or Jacques Plante's legendary mask. Then there are moments that become more significant as time passes. The objects related to these moments become an increasingly valuable part of keeping hockey history alive. And while all moments may not be created equal, everything collected at the Hockey Hall of Fame's D.K. (Doc) Seaman Hockey Resource Centre is treated equally – it's all part of hockey's history, after all.

As far as Phil Pritchard, vice-president and curator of the Hockey Hall of Fame (the man known to most as the "Keeper of the Cup"), is concerned, hockey history is made every day and all over the world, and it is the job of his team at the Resource Centre to collect, catalog and conserve the objects intrinsic to hockey's history.

Take, for instance, an old sweater I found in an arena storage locker in Finland in 1995. I was playing for a team in Finland's fourth highest division (or third lowest, depending on your philosophy). We played our games late at night in front of one or maybe two spectators – a number contingent upon whether any of the players had recently entered a relationship. We had a player-coach.

It's safe to say that no one on the team was going to be inducted into the Hockey Hall of Fame, but we were still making

hockey history – and the sweater I found was certainly part of hockey's history. It was dark blue, like the blue of Team Sweden, and it had five yellow letters running across its chest the same way the Pittsburgh Penguins had "Pittsburgh" back in the 1980s. The five letters were *V*, *O*, *I*, *M* and *A*, spelling *voima*, which means "power" in Finnish.

The sweater was small. Maybe it had shrunk? Maybe players were smaller in the 1970s? Maybe their shoulder pads were even smaller than the ones I was wearing (which weren't much more than two plastic cups stapled to my suspenders)? The fabric of the sweater was wool, not synthetic like the sweaters my team was using. The blue Voima sweater was heavy and tiny and soiled. And that's what the D.K. (Doc) Seaman Hockey Resource Centre identification tag now says. "Blue hockey sweater, with "VOIMA" across the chest. Circa 1970s. Soiled."

Soiled or not, the sweater is a part of the Hockey Hall of Fame collection, adding a piece to the puzzle of the game.

"We're trying to cover the entire game, on all levels, in all countries. Wherever hockey is played, we'd like to be there to record it," says Phil Pritchard.

But how does the staff at the Resource Centre go about obtaining the items in the Hockey Hall of Fame's collection? Because the Hockey Hall of Fame is a registered charity, they typically obtain items for the collection in one of four ways: by personal donation, by anonymous donation (which Pritchard calls "random," as most of these donations come via the daily mail without any identifiers whatsoever), by tracking milestones and special games in

Voima sweater donated to the Hockey Hall of Fame by Finnish hockey player and writer Risto Pakarinen. The sweater was worn during play in Finland's fourth highest division in the 1970s.

the NHL and elsewhere and then asking for the donation when the opportunity arises and, finally, by attending events. Nothing beats being there when you want to get hockey artifacts, like the time Pritchard found himself in the Team Canada dressing room after the men's hockey final at the 2002 Salt Lake Olympics.

"It was pandemonium in there. And in the middle of all of it Wayne Gretzky came over to me and handed me the lucky loonie that was dug out from center ice. He just put it in my hand, looked at me and said, 'On the way back to Canada don't spend this in a pop machine because your whole country is depending on you to get this home!'"

The team at the Resource Centre can't be in every dressing room after every game. However, wherever there's an

International Ice Hockey Federation tournament, the Hockey Hall of Fame is there. Even if none of the staff can be present, the Hall has official and unofficial representatives who can help.

In January 2011, when Team Finland won the bronze-medal game against the Czech Republic in the under-18 women's tournament in Stockholm, Sweden, freelance photographer Matthew

Wayne Gretzky hands Phil Pritchard Team Canada's "lucky loonie" after the men's gold-medal final at the 2002 Winter Olympics. The loonie was placed beneath the ice at the start of the Games by Trent Evans, an ice-maker at the Olympics, and was excavated by Team Canada players following their gold-medal victory.

Murnaghan was quick to approach Team Finland's management to see if he could get some artifacts to take back to the Hall of Fame. He knew what he wanted – something from the team's leading scorer, forward Susanna Tapani. However, having the Hall of Fame grab a glove would have meant that a 17-year-old Finnish girl would have had to buy a new pair of gloves with her own money. So Murnaghan went for the blue helmet, property of the Finnish Ice Hockey Federation, and got an okay from the team manager.

The fact that the Hall of Fame had requested Tapani's helmet was front-page news on the Finnish federation's website the next day. The story also ran in their quarterly magazine. "She's only 17, and already in the Hall of Fame."

Such is the magic of the Hall of Fame.

"It may not look significant at the time, but that helmet we got from the under-18 women's tournament may belong to somebody who will go on to have a great career," says Phil Pritchard.

And the work is never done, as Craig Campbell, Resource Centre manager, attests. "There are absolutely things out there that we'd like to have in our collections," he says. "Our goal is to get at least one artifact from each of our 362 honored members, but we'd love to have something between six and twelve. That way we can honor them here forever. Philosophically, we'd love to have something from every team that's ever played the game. We do it out of passion, to preserve the history of the game well. That's our reward."

Their passion for the game and the reward of preserving its history for future generations are what unites the Hall of Fame and its donors.

For example, the Hockey Hall of Fame has three sweaters worn by Marty Barry, one of the Hall's honored members, who played in the NHL in the 1930s and 1940s and who was nicknamed "Goal-a-game" Barry by local sportswriters. Mr. Barry's daughter and son-in-law decided to donate his sweaters to the Hall of Fame instead of auctioning them off. The Barry sweaters have since been on display not only in the Toronto museum, but also in traveling displays on the East Coast, giving the Barry family a chance to see them, and the people's reaction to them, close to home.

"We're asking people to give up, possibly, their most treasured possessions. Once they get to the museum and see how everything is presented and preserved, and realize it will always be available for the general public to see, they know they've made the right choice," says Phil Pritchard.

Campbell concurs: "If somebody has a sweater, a program collection or a photo collection, and we inquire about it for donation, it means a lot to them that the Hockey Hall of Fame calls. They may have spent their life trying to capture the game for the local team or media and maybe they want to leave a legacy here."

Just as Jack and Peter Mecca did. The relationship between the Hall and the brother photographers started when Campbell found a slide of Philadelphia Flyers forward Bill Barber. On the slide were the names Jack and Peter Mecca. Campbell managed to get in touch with Jack and explained to the former photographer that the Hall of Fame would be interested in preserving any images he and his brother still had.

It turned out that the Mecca brothers had a bunch of photos. The two ran a hockey magazine of their own, called *Hockey*, in the 1970s, and they also shot games for other publications, such as *Time*. Jack donated the photos to the Hall of Fame, where the collection was organized and preserved. He and his family then visited the Hall to see his and his brother's legacy.

"It was a powerful moment. Jack is very proud that the Mecca collection is now at the Hall of Fame, helping us preserve the history of the game," Craig Campbell says.

But donors and NHL players can be reluctant to part with their treasures. Steve Poirier, coordinator of the Hockey Hall of Fame images and archival services, attended the 2011 NHL All-Star Game in Carolina and asked superstar winger Alex Ovechkin what he was willing to donate to the Hall. "Ovechkin wanted to keep almost everything, but he did give me the Carolina Hurricanes flip-flops he had worn his entire time in Raleigh," Poirier said, laughing.

But, as Miragh Bitove, the archivist and collections registrar, insists, "We're hockey's archeologists. If we find half a clay pot, well, it's half a clay pot more than we had before."

And that is the point. Whether it is Alex Ovechkin of the Washington Capitals wearing Carolina Hurricanes flip-flops for an All-Star weekend or the helmet of a promising teenage girl from Finland, everything is important and has its place.

A great example of a rare and unlikely artifact is one of Bitove's personal favorites from the collection: "We have a Mexican flag from the 1928 Olympics. A family member called us and said that their father was on the Canadian team and that, after their last game, he had climbed up the flagpole and stolen the Mexican flag on a dare. It was also the first year that Mexico participated in the Winter Olympics, so that's a little special, but for me, the fun part is imagining the 20-year-olds daring each other to do it," she says.

Another great story involves Hobey Baker, the only American among 12 original inductees into the Hockey Hall of Fame in 1945. Baker was a multi-sport talent who played both football and hockey for Princeton University in the early 20th century and died tragically when his plane crashed during a test flight, right after World War I.

"A woman told me that her grandfather had been a farmhand for the Baker's in Pennsylvania. When he left work at the farm, the family gave him some of the trophies that Hobey and his brother Thornton Baker had won in school," says Bitove. Today the Hobey Baker Award is awarded annually to the best player in NCAA hockey.

The revolving, high-density shelving at the Resource Centre houses items in the archives when they aren't on display at the Hall or part of a traveling exhibit. Currently they contain more than 26,000 published hockey books, programs and guides; approximately 10,000 individual player files (including photos, contracts and other ephemera); close to 10,000 individual team, league and trophy files; more than 450 binders of hockey cards, tickets and schedules; and more than 1 million negatives and slides, 32,000 photographs and 4,000 film reels. The collection

also contains 4,000 hockey sticks, more than 1,500 jerseys and over 3,000 pieces of equipment – and counting.

It wasn't always this way. When Phil Pritchard started at the Hockey Hall of Fame 25 years ago, it was housed in the 7,500-square-foot premises at the Canadian National Exhibition (CNE) in Toronto, Ontario, which had opened there in 1961. While there, Pritchard would use the exhibition grounds to expand the reach of the collection, physically and emotionally, by having outdoor displays and competitions for the fair visitors. For many in the region, an annual summer ritual was to go to the CNE and, while there, visit the Hockey Hall of Fame.

In 1993 the Hall of Fame moved to its current location, the former Bank of Montreal building at the corner of Yonge Street and Front Street in the heart of Toronto. This heritage building is part of a larger property called Brookfield Place, and the Hockey Hall of Fame is firmly entrenched as a marquee proprietor, covering almost 60,000 square feet of exhibition space – eight times larger than the former CNE space. But even that was too small to house everything. To alleviate the problem, the Hall used off-site storage, but this posed logistical problems and made it difficult to access important artifacts quickly and easily.

Recognizing the need for a dedicated home for the archival collection, Hockey Hall of Fame chairman Bill Hay and president Jeff Denomme spearheaded the creation of the 18,000-square-foot state-of-the-art D.K. (Doc) Seaman Hockey Resource Centre (named in honor of the late Daryl K. (Doc) Seaman, one of the founding owners of the Calgary Flames). The move to the dedicated facility in 2009 not only gave Pritchard and his team room to operate, it gave them room to grow the collection. The move also created more exhibition and office space at the Hockey Hall of Fame, enabling operations staff to reclaim much-needed space.

"The Resource Centre allows us to consolidate our collections into a single satellite operation to better serve our principal museum attraction, which continues to flourish at Brookfield Place," Pritchard said.

FROM DONATION TO EXHIBITION
The Life of an Artifact

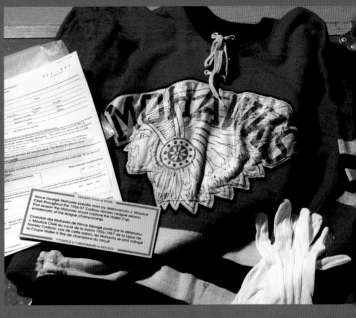

▲ This Prince George Mohawks sweater, worn by donor J. Maurice Clark throughout the 1956–57 Cariboo Hockey League season, sits with some key components used by the Hockey Hall of Fame to preserve and showcase hockey artifacts. These include a travel case, display placard, article registration form, plastic archival bag and white archival gloves.

STEP ONE: DONATION   The Hockey Hall of Fame's collection is acquired through donation. Items can be donated to the Hall of Fame through the mail or in person at the Hall, the D.K. (Doc) Seaman Hockey Resource Centre or any touring exhibit. Hall of Fame staff also collect artifacts at hockey events. Donors can receive a tax receipt for the estimated worth of the donation. Appraisals are done by a third-party contracted by the Hockey Hall of Fame.

STEP TWO: CATALOGING AND DOCUMENTATION   Once an item is donated, it is sent to the archivist and collections registrar, who catalogs the item in a digital database. The archivist and collections registrar also creates an identification document that stays with the artifact. The document lists the donor, the appearance and condition of the item, as well as its history. If the item's history is unknown, the archivist and collections registrar will conduct research and attempt to uncover the origin of the artifact. Oftentimes, photos will be taken of new donations for the "Recent Acquisitions" feature in the Hockey Hall of Fame's quarterly news and events journal, *Teammates*, and its annual program, *Legends*.

STEP THREE: PRESERVATION   Preservation involves textile freezing and bagging: artifacts are bagged in clear plastic for protection and are then frozen. Freezing eliminates bugs and bacteria that can deteriorate an artifact. Donated items are seldom washed or cleaned, so freezing is essential to ensure the longevity of an artifact. After an artifact has been handled outside of the bag, or been on display, it is frozen again.

STEP FOUR: RACKING   After preservation, artifacts are placed in a climate-controlled archive that stays at 64ºF to 68ºF (18ºC to 20ºC), with 40 percent humidity, for paper and textiles and 54ºF to 58ºF (12ºC to 15ºC), with 40 percent humidity, for film and magnetic materials. Each item is classified and racked according to its classification (for example, International Hockey>World Championships>Finland).

STEP FIVE: EXHIBITION   Items are selected for one of many exhibition platforms and are packed in heavy-duty trunks to protect them during transport. A variety of custom-made, artifact-friendly props are used to display the artifacts once on exhibit, and Hall staff wear white archival gloves while handling any artifact.

The dedicated archive building also provides historians and authors with a place to conduct research and gives hockey nuts a chance to book tours to see the state-of-the-art facility. Most importantly, the Resource Centre allows the Hall of Fame to really concentrate on and build upon their outreach program, in which the Hall arranges road shows, taking selected parts of their collection to the public.

"Our outreach program covers everything that we take on the road. Traveling exhibits, temporary exhibits or loans that can last up to a year, including our interactive games, the trophies and artwork," says Izak Westgate, manager of the outreach exhibits and assistant curator.

The Hall of Fame works in conjunction with teams, leagues and federations to create exhibits that showcase the Hall of Fame and celebrate the league or area the exhibit is visiting. Not everybody can get to Toronto, but the outreach program gives the public a chance to see some of the Hall's collection. Getting the collection on the road to different locations ensures that different items are presented to as many people as possible. It also gets the staff out on the road, and you never know whom you're going to meet or what you're going to find once you're out there.

"When we sell the Hall, it comes from the heart. We talk from our heart to their hearts and hope that they share our belief that it is important to be able to show these wonderful artifacts to the general public," says Phil Pritchard.

And lets not forget the Stanley Cup, which travels with Pritchard or one of a select few Cup Keepers, over 300 days a year. It is one of the world's most recognizable trophies, and it gets a lot of attention.

"The great thing about the Cup is that no matter how many times you've seen it, it still sends a little chill down your spine. That is what makes it the greatest trophy in sports. It's special," says Pritchard, who has had some pretty special moments with Stanley. In the summer of 2009, Pritchard, the Stanley Cup and the Prince of Wales Trophy (given to the Eastern Conference playoff champion) were on a boat in the middle of Lake Michigan salmon fishing with Pittsburgh Penguins coach Dan Bylsma.

By noon they'd already caught over 600 pounds of salmon. Who knew Lord Stanley was a fisherman?

"In the beginning, we didn't know what our role in the hockey world was," says Craig Campbell. "Both Phil and I collected things as kids, and I guess that nature of collecting and archiving has become our life here."

So, pieces of hockey's history are added, daily, to the Hockey Hall of Fame collection. Some donated items belong to the capital *M* moments, and others, like the sweater from Finland that I donated, help flesh out the rest of hockey's story. That sweater, by the way, was most likely worn by defenseman Eino Niiranen in Finland's fourth highest division in the 1970s. Niiranen's nickname was "Nakki," which means, "sausage," and it was bestowed upon the stocky rearguard for obvious reasons, but he was a key player on the team's blueline. He was also a key person for the Voima club, staying on as a trainer and all-round helper after his own career as a player came to an end. He finally ended up as the team statistician. (And, curiously, in the morning paper the day after a game there was always a Voima story penned by the mysterious "N.")

Nakki kept the club alive and, with it, kept a small community alive and vibrant. Phil Pritchard knows the Nakkis of the world, and while they may never be inducted into the Hockey Hall of Fame, the game wouldn't be anything without them.

"We salute those that have made the game great," says Pritchard. "We're only as good as our past and present."

RISTO PAKARINEN is an author and hockey journalist from Finland. He is a regular contributor to *The Hockey News* and has been published in *ESPN The Magazine, The Sporting News* and *Fast Company,* as well as on ESPN.com, NHL.com and IIHF.com.

ACKNOWLEDGMENTS

Hockey Hall of Fame Treasures is a truly unique book, and its creation would not have been possible without the contributions of the following people, whom I would like to recognize and thank:

Matthew Manor, for your excellent attitude, easygoing nature, great photographic eye and ability to work on the fly under many different circumstances. Thank you for being your own grip, best boy and carpenter – a true one-man show! As well, thanks for sharing your creative input, you are an art director's best friend.

Phil Pritchard, Craig Campbell, Miragh Bitove, Steve Poirier, Izak Westgate, Kirt Berry, Anna Presta and Bill Wellman at the Hockey Hall of Fame Resource Centre, as well as Peter Jagla, Craig Baines, Tome Geneski, Tyler Wolosewich, Scott Veber and Pearl Rajwanth at the Hockey Hall of Fame. Thank you for your patience, knowledge and support and for providing me ready access to the collection.

Linda Gustafson and Peter Ross of Counterpunch Design, for your commitment to great book design. From the initial stages to the finished product, you both treated this book like you had no others to work on. Thank you. Your design has captured the true spirit of what I envisioned for this book.

Special thanks to: Scotty Bowman, Nancy Foran, Darryl Boynton, Steve Milton, Sarah Chisnall and her crew at the MasterCard Centre for Hockey Excellence; Henning Svendsen and the Toronto Marlies, for unfettered access to the team's practice facility; Claudine Mersereau, for your patience and honest opinion; Michael Worek, for being the best sounding board there ever was; Lionel Koffler, Jacqueline Hope-Raynor, Hartley Millson, Rachel Thompson and the rest of my great colleagues at Firefly Books; Jennifer Malloy at Moveable Type; as well as the staff of the Hockey Hall of Fame: Bill Hay, Jeff Denomme, Ron Ellis, Darren Boyko, Kelly Masse, Jackie Schwartz, Wendy Cramer, Joshua Dawson, Joanna White, Craig Beckim, Steve Ozimec, Patrick Minogue, Dwayne Schrader, Mike Briggs, Sarah Lee, Anthony Fusco, Sandra Walters, Chris Chu, Arlyn Fortin, Sylvia Lau, Sarah Talbot and the maintenance crew (especially those who stayed overnight on photo shoots).

Lastly, thanks to all of those who, over the years, have made the Hockey Hall of Fame one of the most special places on earth.

STEVE CAMERON, editor

Steve Cameron asked me to help create his vision for this book. Without the support and contributions of many people, that vision could never have been realized. First I would like to thank all the staff at the Hockey Hall of Fame and the Hockey Hall of Fame Resource Centre. Their efforts made it possible for us to create each and every image, giving the archival collection the respect it deserves. Also, thank you to the staff of the MasterCard Centre and the Toronto Marlies. Both organizations gave us exceptional access to their facilities, enabling us to create unique images of artifacts in their natural environment. Thank you to my parents, Ron and Barb, for their guidance, love and support throughout my childhood and adult life. You made me into the man I am today and gave me the passion to pursue my dreams. Thanks to my brother, Scott, and my grandfather A.J. Stevenson. My love of this game comes from you. Of course, a very special thanks to my partner in life, my wife, Jessica, and my beautiful girls, Sophie and Ruby. Your love, support and understanding inspire me to strive for the best in every day and have helped me accomplish things I never knew I could. I can only hope I do the same for you.

MATTHEW MANOR, photographer

EXTENDED CAPTIONS

Pages 46–47

1 Mike Gartner's 1987 Canada Cup jersey, worn during Game 3 of the final at Copps Coliseum in Hamilton, Ontario, where Team Canada defeated the Russians in a thrilling 6–5 victory for the championship.

2 Team Canada 74 jersey worn by WHA superstar Bobby Hull. Team Canada's fate would not be as good as that of Team Canada 72, with the Russians taking the eight game series with a 4–1–3 record.

3 Winnipeg Monarchs Team Canada sweater from the 1935 World Championship in Switzerland. The Allan Cup–winning Moncton Hawks couldn't afford to make the trip, so the Monarchs, the 1934 Manitoba champions, represented Canada. The Monarchs won the Worlds undefeated.

4 Theoren Fleury's Team Canada jersey from the 2002 Winter Olympics. Fleury overcame a turbulent first half to his 2001–02 NHL season and joined Canada to compete at his second Olympic Games, earning a gold medal.

5 Edmonton Mercurys sweater worn by Harry Allen during the 1950 World Championship. The Mercurys won all seven games they played by a combined score of 42–3, capturing Canada's 13th World Championship.

6 Sudbury Wolves Team Canada sweater worn by Herb Kewley at the 1949 World Championship. It was Canada's first appearance at the Worlds since 1939. Canada finished runner-up to Czechoslovakia, loosing 3–2 in the final.

7 Whitby Dunlops sweater worn by defenseman and team captain Harry Sinden while representing Canada at the 1958 World Championship. The Dunnies won all seven games to capture Canada's first gold since 1955.

8 Penticton Vees Team Canada sweater worn by goaltender Ivan McLelland at the 1955 World Championship. Canada defeated the newly formed Soviet Union squad 5–0 on the final day of the tournament to earn the gold medal.

Page 52

1 Jean Béliveau's 380th goal puck, which placed him third in NHL career goals. He scored it on March 2, 1966, at Maple Leaf Gardens.

2 Final puck from Kim St. Pierre's performance as the first female goalie to win a game in men's Canadian Interuniversity Sport play. St. Pierre's McGill Redmen beat the Ryerson Rams 5–2 on November 15, 2003.

3 The third-goal puck from Wayne Gretzky's first NHL hat trick, scored on February 1, 1980.

4 Puck used by Quinnipiac University's Greg Holt on March 12, 2010, to end the longest hockey game in NCAA history. Holt's marker came against Union College at 10:22 in the fifth overtime.

5 Puck used by Justin Magnuson to score the championship-winning goal for Team Saskatchewan over Team Manitoba at the 2003 National Aboriginal Hockey Championship.

6 Shorthanded-goal puck fired by Detroit's Chris Chelios on April 21, 2007, against the Calgary Flames; the 45-year-old Chelios became the oldest player in NHL history to score a shorthanded goal.

7 Puck Michel Goulet used to score his 1,000th point, on February 23, 1991, against the Minnesota North Stars. Goulet was the 30th player in NHL history to reach that plateau.

8 Puck from career-goal 718 by Detroit's Brett Hull, scored against the St. Louis Blues on October 29, 2003. The goal placed Hull fourth overall on the NHL career-goal list.

9 Borden Smith of the Eastern Hockey League's Clinton Comets scored his 50th goal of the 1967–68 season with this puck. Smith finished with a club-record 69 goals, a career high.

Pages 58–59

1   Stick used by Boston's John Bucyk to score his 500th NHL goal, scored on October 30, 1975, against the St. Louis Blues.

2   Dany Heatley of the Ottawa Senators used this stick on October 5, 2005, to score the goal that clinched the first shoot-out in NHL history.

3   Sweden's Michael Nylander used this stick at the 1997 World Championship, where he recorded 11 points in 11 games and was named the tournament's top forward.

4   Jean Ratelle of the New York Rangers scored his 250th goal with this stick on January 28, 1973, in a 5–2 win over the Toronto Maple Leafs.

5   Brad Park's Christian from the early 1980s. Park, while with the Detroit Red Wings, became the first NHL player to use an aluminum-shafted stick when he began using this model of Christian.

6   Stick used by Mike Bossy to score his 300th NHL goal, on March 23, 1982. The goal made Bossy the youngest to reach that milestone, and it was part of four-goal night in an 8–1 romp of the Washington Capitals.

7   Don Parsons of the United Hockey League's Quad City Mallards scored his 623rd professional goal with this stick on March 24, 2007. The goal made Parsons the top-scoring American in professional hockey.

8   Andy Bathgate of the New York Rangers used this Northland to pot his 200th career goal during the 1961–62 NHL season; he ended with a league-high 56 assists and 84 points.

9   Kevin Kerr of the UHL's Flint Generals used this blacked-out composite-shaft stick to score his 664th pro goal, a minor-pro record, on January 7, 2005.

10 Darren Haydar of the AHL's Chicago Wolves netted his 52nd career playoff goal and 120th career playoff point with this stick during Game 2 of the 2008 Calder Cup final, setting two AHL records.

11 Kelly Bechard of Calgary's Oval X-Treme used this stick to score the championship-winning goal against the Brampton Thunder in the 2004 National Women's Hockey League final.

12 Stick used by Don Luce to score his 33rd goal of the 1974–75 season. Luce and five other Buffalo Sabres scored 30 or more goals that season, setting an NHL record for the number of players with 30 or more goals from the same club.

13 Canada's Glenn Anderson used this stick at the 1989 World Championship; Canada took home silver.

14 Valeri Kharlamov's stick from the infamous meeting between the Philadelphia Flyers and the Red Army on January 11, 1976, when the Red Army team protested the violence of the Flyers by staging a walkout.

15 Braden Pimm of the British Columbia Hockey League's Vernon Vipers scored the championship-wining goal of the 2009 RBC Cup with this stick.

Pages 60–61

1   Percy LeSueur's famous one-piece wood stick, used from 1906–09. This stick saw action with both his Smith Falls, Ontario, club team and the Ottawa Senators, with whom LeSueur won the Stanley Cup in 1906 and 1909. LeSueur engraved his stick with his name and the dates and scores of his Stanley Cup challenges.

2   Harry "Hap" Holmes used this one-piece wood stick while with the Victoria Cougars. The team won the 1924–25 Stanley Cup, becoming the last non-NHL team to with the Cup. Holmes had his entire team autograph his stick.

3   Scott Clemmensen of the Boston College Eagles used this stick to capture the 2001 NCAA Frozen Four final and was named top goalie of the tournament.

4   Arturs Irbe used this blacked-out Sher-Wood while representing Latvia at the 1997 World Championship.

5   New Jersey's Glenn Resch used this prototype "Curtis Curve" stick (made with a curve where the shaft meets the paddle) to record his 200th career win on October 12, 1984, against the New York Islanders.

6   Ari Sulander of Finland used this stick while backstopping his team to the silver medal at the 1998 World Championship.

7   Toronto's Terry Sawchuk blanked the Chicago Black Hawks with this stick on March 4, 1967, to claim his 100th career shutout.

8   Stick used by Carson Chubak of the Prince Albert Mintos to help capture the 2007 Telus Cup (Canada's national midget championship), making the Mintos the first-ever back-to-back champions.

9   Kyle Gajewski used this Eagle stick with a custom finger groove in the paddle to help Team Ontario win the 2004 World Under-17 Championship.

10 Phoenix's Brian Boucher set two modern-day NHL records with this stick in January 2004 by posting five consecutive shutouts and playing 332:01 minutes of goal-less hockey.

11 Nikolai Khabibulin notched his 300th career win with this stick as the Edmonton Oilers defeated the Dallas Stars in a 5–4 shoot-out victory on October 6, 2009.

12 Tony Esposito used this stick to collect his 76th, and final, career shutout on January 15, 1984, in a 2–0 win over Pittsburgh.

13 Stick used by Charline Labonté of the Montreal Axion to post a shutout to help claim the 2006 National Women's Hockey League title. Labonté was also named tournament MVP.

14 Josh Harding used this Sher-Wood in the 2002 World Under-18 Championship, Canada's first-ever entry in the tournament. The team finished sixth.

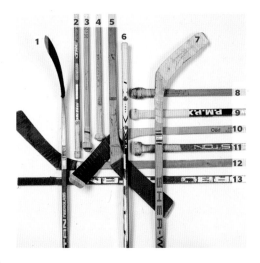

Page 64

1   Philadelphia's Rick MacLeish became the first expansion team player to post a 50-goal season after scoring against the Pittsburgh Penguins with this stick on April 1, 1973.

2   Stick used by Boston's Phil Esposito on February 20, 1971, to become the fourth player in NHL history to score 50 goals in a season.

3   Stick used by Buffalo star Rick Martin to record a hat trick, including the game winner, during a 5–2 victory over St. Louis on April 7, 1974. The first of Martin's goals was also his 50th, making him the first Sabre to reach that milestone.

4   Atlanta's Guy Chouinard scored his 50th goal of the 1978–79 season with this stick during a 9–2 victory over the New York Rangers.

5   Stick used by captain Rick Vaive in a 4–3 win against St. Louis on March 24, 1982, when he became the first Toronto Maple Leaf to score 50 goals in a single season.

6   Jean Pronovost used this stick to become the first Pittsburgh Penguin in franchise history to record 50 goals in a season, when he beat Boston netminder Gilles Gilbert during a 5–5 tie on March 24, 1976.

7   Atlanta Thrashers superstar Ilya Kovalchuk used this stick on March 18, 2008, to record his 50th goal of the season, the second time he reached that plateau.

8   Stick used by sniper Mike Bossy of the New York Islanders on April 1, 1978, in a game against the Washington Capitals, when he became the first NHL rookie, and third youngest player, to reach the 50-goal mark.

9   Rangers captain Vic Hadfield used this stick to score two goals during the final game of the 1971–72 season, becoming the first Ranger and the sixth player in NHL history to score 50 goals in a season.

10 Stick used by Paul Jackson of the Central Hockey League's Wichita Thunder to score his 50th goal in 37 games on January 14, 1994. Jackson finished the season with a league-record 71 goals.

11 Washington's Bobby Carpenter became the first U.S.-born player to score 50 goals in a single season when he used this stick to beat Montreal netminder Steve Penney on March 21, 1985.

12 Calgary star Lanny McDonald used this stick to become the first player of the 1982–83 NHL season to reach 50 goals, on February 18, 1983.

13 Alex Ovechkin hit the 50-goal mark for the first time with this stick on March 3, 2008, in a 10–2 romp of the Boston Bruins. The superstar winger notched a hat trick and five points on the night.

14 On March 26, 1988, LA Kings forward Jimmy Carson used this stick to become the second-youngest player in NHL history to record a 50-goal season.

15 Stick used by LA's Luc Robitaille to record his first 50-goal season during a 6–3 victory over the Calgary Flames on April 1, 1988.

Page 65

1   Stick used by Mario Lemieux during the 1988 NHL All-Star Game in St. Louis, Missouri. Lemieux collected six points, an All-Star record, including the overtime winning goal.

2   Canadian forward Jayna Hefford used this stick to score the gold-medal-winning goal at the 2002 Winter Olympics, as Canada defeated the United States 3–2.

3   Stick used by Jean Béliveau on February 1, 1969, to score his 450th career goal. He became the third player, behind Gordie Howe and Maurice Richard, to reach that milestone.

4   Montreal's Frank Mahovlich used this stick to pot the game-winning goal against Vancouver on March 21, 1973, clinching the East Division for the Habs and collecting his 500th career tally, the fifth NHLer to do so.

5   Bill Barilko of the Toronto Maple Leafs used this stick to score the famed triple-overtime Stanley Cup–winning goal on April 21, 1951, against Gerry McNeil of the Montreal Canadiens.

6   Stick used by Canadian forward Jarome Iginla to assist on Sidney Crosby's gold-medal-winning goal at the 2010 Winter Olympics. It was the second time Iginla had assisted on an Olympic gold-medal-winning goal.

7   The stick George Morrison used as a member of the Minnesota Fighting Saints to set a WHA record by scoring three goals in 43 seconds on April 3, 1974, versus the Vancouver Blazers.

8   On October 23, 1966, Bobby Orr borrowed this stick from Boston teammate Bob Dillabough and used it to score his first NHL goal.

9   Petr Svoboda of the Czech Republic used this stick to score the lone goal in a 1–0 victory over Russia in the gold-medal game of the 1998 Winter Olympics.

10 On March 30, during the final game of the 1968–69 season, Bobby Hull used this stick to score his 58th goal of the season in a 9–5 victory over the Detroit Red Wings. Hull's 58 goals set an NHL single-season scoring record.

11 Stick used by New York's Brian Leetch to score the only Ranger goal in a 2–1 overtime loss to the Pittsburgh Penguins on April 18, 1999. The goal marked the final assist (1,963) and final point (2,857) of Wayne Gretzky's legendary career.

12 Last stick used by Toronto's Ace Bailey. He used it in a December 12, 1933, contest during which he suffered a career-ending head injury. The first NHL All-Star Game was played two months later, as a benefit for Bailey.

13 Mike Bossy scored the 400th goal of his career with this stick on January 14, 1984. Bossy became the quickest in NHL history to reach 400 goals, recording the milestone in only his 506th career game.

Page 68

1 Laura Hurd of the Elmira College Soaring Eagles wore these gloves during the 2001–02 season, during which she scored the championship-winning goal of the inaugural NCAA Division III National Women's Tournament.

2 Cooper gloves worn by Boston's Terry O'Reilly. O'Reilly spent his entire 14-year NHL career in Boston and likely started wearing these gloves in 1973 and wore them for more than one season.

3 Superstar Joe Sakic wore these gloves during a portion of the 2006–07 NHL season, including a February 15 game in Calgary that saw him record five points, including two goals, the second of which was the 600th goal of his illustrious career.

4 The gloves Scott Stevens wore throughout the 2003 playoffs, when his New Jersey Devils defeated the Anaheim Mighty Ducks to claim his and the club's third Stanley Cup.

5 Gloves worn by Luc Robitaille of the LA Kings during the 1993–94 season, which he finished with 44 goals and 42 assists for 86 points.

6 Scott Niedermayer of the New Jersey Devils wore these gloves to assist on Neal Broten's Stanley Cup–winning goal as the Devils swept the Detroit Red Wings in 1995 to win their first championship in franchise history.

7 Tampa Bay's Dave Andreychuk wore these gloves while playing in his first Stanley Cup final. Andreychuk snapped his unofficial record of playing the most games (1,759) without winning the Cup when Tampa defeated the Calgary Flames in seven games on June 7, 2004.

8 Brian Rolston wore these gloves during the 2006–07 season; he led the charge as his Minnesota Wild made the playoffs for the first time since 2003. Rolston led the Wild in both goals (31) and points (64).

Page 69

1 Gloves worn by Pat LaFontaine during the 1992–93 season, the best statistical season of his NHL career. LaFontaine led the Buffalo Sabres with 95 assists and 148 points and was named a Second Team All-Star.

2 Defenseman Guy Lapointe, a four-time NHL All-Star and six-time Cup winner during 14 seasons with the Montreal Canadiens, wore these gloves during his final years with the Habs, in the early 1980s.

3 Steve Poirier wore these black-and-white leather Cooper gloves between 1991 and 1993 as a member of the Alexandria Glens in the Eastern Ontario Junior B Hockey League.

4 Tampa Bay Lightning rookie Steven Stamkos wore these gloves while participating in the 2009 NHL YoungStars Game during All-Star weekend in Montreal, Quebec, recording two goals.

5 Gloves used by Cam Neely of the Boston Bruins at the 1996 NHL All-Star Game in Boston. This was Neely's fifth All-Star Game appearance.

6 Gloves worn by Trevor Jobe of the ECHL's Nashville Knights to score 50 goals in 37 games in 1992–93. That season Jobe set new league records for goals (85) and points (161) and was named the ECHL's MVP.

7 Jet Fumerton of the Creston Jets wore these gloves for approximately 20 years, from the mid-1970s until the mid-1990s, during senior women's play in British Columbia.

8 Gloves worn by Wendel Clark of the Quebec Nordiques during the 1994–95 NHL season, his only season with the club and the franchise's last season in Quebec City.

9 Detroit's Larry Murphy wore these gloves throughout the 2000–01 NHL season, his 21st and final year. Murphy retired second all-time in NHL games played (1,615) and finished third all-time in points by a defenseman (1,216).

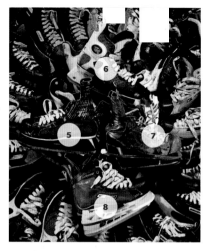
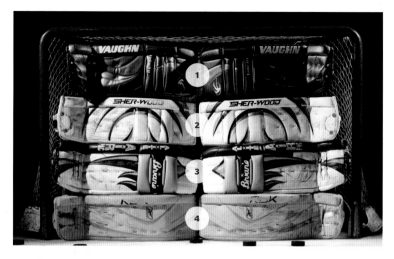

Page 80

1 Skates worn by All-Star left winger Frank Mahovlich. He was chosen for First or Second All-Star Teams an impressive nine times during his career.

2 Evgeni Malkin wore these skates for much of 2005 and 2006, using them to compete in the 2005–06 Russian Super League season, the 2006 World Junior Championship, the 2006 Winter Olympics, the 2006 World Championship and for the start of the 2006–07 NHL season.

3 Skates worn by Hall of Famer Clint Smith for a portion of his 11-year NHL career, which spanned 1936–47.

4 Tampa Bay Lightning alternate captain Vincent Lecavalier wore these skates during the second half of the 2006–07 NHL season, his only season to top 50 goals and 100 points.

Page 81

5 Retired referee Frank Udvari borrowed these skates from Bryan Trottier on December 30, 1978, when he replaced injured referee Dave Newell during first period action between the Atlanta Flames and the New York Islanders. Udvari called two penalties and disallowed a goal scored by Trottier.

6 Skates worn by Edmonton Oilers alternate captain Ryan Smyth during the 2002–03 NHL season and the 2003 World Championship. Smyth captained Team Canada to its first Worlds gold medal since 1997.

7 Skates worn by Bobby Clarke of the Flin Flon Bombers during his final season of Western Canadian Hockey League action, in 1968–69. Clarke led the league in scoring, with 137 points, and was named MVP as the Bombers captured the league championship.

8 Jinelle Zaugg wore these skates while playing for the University of Wisconsin Badgers during the 2006–07 NCAA women's regular season and playoffs, when the Badgers won their second of four national championships.

Page 97

1 Mike D'Alessandro of the University of Western Ontario Mustangs wore these pads during the 2001–02 Ontario University Athletics season, the 2002 OUA Queen's Cup tournament and the 2002 Canadian Interuniversity Sport University Cup tournament. The team went undefeated during the OUA regular season, with D'Alessandro leading the OUA in both goals-against average (1.25) and save percentage (0.925%).

2 Jocelyn Thibault of the Pittsburgh Penguins wore these pads during the end of the 2006–07 NHL regular season and playoffs. The Penguins finished the regular season in second place in the NHL's Atlantic Division of the Eastern Conference.

3 Goalie pads worn by Mike Dunham of the Nashville Predators during their inaugural NHL season, in 1998–99. Dunham played in the Predators' first game, on October 10, 1998, at the Gaylord Entertainment Center in Nashville – a 1–0 loss to the Florida Panthers.

4 Yellow goalie pads worn by Marc-André Fleury of the Pittsburgh Penguins throughout the 2006–07 season. Fleury recorded a career-high five shutouts in the regular season.

Page 108

STALL 1

(Gloves) Gloves worn by Marion Pepels of the Netherlands throughout the 2003 Women's World Championship Division II tournament in Lecco, Italy, as well as throughout her lengthy club-team career with EV Zug/Seewen.

(Helmet) Helmet painted in Die Adler Mannheim colors and logos, worn by Markus Wieland during the first half of the 1999–2000 German Ice Hockey League season.

(Jersey) Vaasan Sport jersey worn by longtime Finnish star Sari Krooks throughout the 1993–94 Finnish Women's National League season.

(Pants) Swedish defender Gunilla Andersson wore these pants throughout the 2006 Winter Olympics. Her six points tied for the tournament lead, as Sweden upset Team USA 3–2 in the semifinal en route to capturing the silver medal.

(Socks) Finnish defenseman Aki-Petteri Berg's socks, worn during the men's bronze-medal game at the 1998 Winter Olympics. Finland won the bronze, defeating Canada by a score of 3–2.

(Skates) Russian forward Maxim Sushinsky wore these skates while helping lead his country to the 2008 World Championship gold medal, Russia's first in 15 years.

STALL 2

(Gloves) Juan Pablo Roberts wore these Mexican National Team gloves during the 2000 D Pool World Championship. Roberts, who had formerly played Junior A hockey in Ontario, recorded three points during Mexico's inaugural senior international tournament, a seventh place finish.

(Helmet) Emma Laaksonen wore this Finnish National Team helmet during the 2000 Women's World Championship. Finland went on to defeat Sweden 7–1 in the bronze-medal game.

(Pants) Aki-Petteri Berg's pants, worn while he was playing defense for Finland at the 1998 Winter Olympics in Nagano, Japan.

(Jersey) South African National Team jersey worn by Jack Valadas at the 2008 Men's Division III World Championship. Valadas, South Africa's top scorer, finished 12th overall in tournament points.

(Socks) Peter Forsberg's socks, worn while representing Sweden at the 1998 Winter Olympics.

(Skates) Skates worn by Valeri Shyryaev during the 2003–04 Swiss A National League season while playing for SC Bern, who captured the Swiss national title.

Page 109

STALL 3

(Gloves) Gloves worn by Team Canada's Jayna Hefford during the 2002 Winter Olympics. Hefford would record her second game-winning goal of the tournament during a 3–2 victory over the U.S. in the gold-medal game.

(Helmet) Gábor Ocskay wore this Hungarian National Team helmet while leading the 2002 Division I Group B World Championship tournament in scoring, with nine points. Hungary earned the silver medal.

(Jersey) Kazakhstan National Team jersey worn by netminder Vitaliy Kolesnik during the 2005 World Championship. Kazakhstan finished 12th, the country's best finish at the tournament.

(Pants) A sample pair of pants that the Canadian National Women's Team wore during the 1990 Women's World Championship, the first ever held. Canada defeated the United States for the gold medal.

(Socks) Wesley Snell wore these socks during the 1997–98 Swiss National B League season while playing for SC Langnau. Langnau won the B League final as well as two postseason qualification games, allowing the club to move up to A League status for the next season.

(Skates) Skates worn by Hamburg Freezers star forward Brad Purdie throughout the 2003–04 German National League season. Purdie led the Freezers in scoring and finished fifth in the league, with 52 points.

STALL 4

(Gloves) Gloves worn by German National Team member Sascha Goc at the 1998 World Championship.

(Helmet) Helmet worn by the Swedish Elite League's leading goal-scorer, Jörgen Jönsson of Färjestad BK, during the 2001–02 season. Jönsson and Färjestad swept Modo in the final to capture their first Swedish title since 1998.

(Pants) Pants worn by Canadian forward Nancy Drolet during the 2001 Women's World Championship. Drolet led the tournament in scoring, with 11 points, helping Canada capture their seventh consecutive gold medal.

(Jersey) Team Netherlands jersey worn by George Peternousek. Between 1978 and 1989 the Dutch won the B Pool World Championship once and the C Pool tournament three times.

(Socks) Czech National Team socks worn by Ales Hemsky throughout the 2006 Winter Olympic Games, where the Czechs finished third.

(Skates) Skates worn by Herb Kewley as a member of the Sudbury Cubs senior club that represented Canada at the 1949 World Championship, where they captured a silver medal.

Pages 118–119

1 Dave Keon scored his 250th career goal with this stick on December 30, 1970, during the Toronto Maple Leafs' 3–1 victory over goaltender Gary Smith and the California Golden Seals.

2 Stick used by Detroit's Ted Lindsay on December 21, 1952, to beat New York Rangers goalie Chuck Rayner for his 200th career goal.

3 On April 4, 1976, Montreal's Guy Lafleur used this stick to score his 56th goal of the season and his 125th point, setting new club records as well as a new NHL record for points in a single season by a right winger.

4 Mario Lemieux recorded his 65th goal of the 1987–88 NHL season with this stick. Lemieux would finish the year with 70 goals, becoming just the fourth NHL player to reach that mark.

5 Gordie Howe of the Detroit Red Wings tied Maurice "Rocket" Richard for the NHL's all-time goal-scoring lead when he potted his 544th goal past Montreal's Gump Worsley with this stick on October 27, 1963.

6 On January 4, 1992, New York Rangers winger Mike Gartner used this stick to score his 1,000th NHL career point, making him the 33rd player to reach that milestone.

7 Stick used by Team Canada forward Paul Henderson to slip a puck under Soviet netminder Vladislav Tretiak with 34 seconds remaining in the eighth and final game of the 1972 Summit Series. The goal gave Canada a 6–5 lead in the game and a 4–3–1 series victory.

8 During the final game of the 1990–91 NHL season, St. Louis Blues sniper Brett Hull used this stick to score his 86th goal of the year, the third highest total in NHL history, behind only Wayne Gretzky (92 and 87).

9 Montreal's "Rocket" Richard used this stick to become the NHL's all-time leading goal scorer on November 8, 1952, when he swiped a puck past Chicago's Al Rollins to record his 325th career goal, surpassing the previous record held by Nels Stewart.

10 One of a few sticks used by Toronto Maple Leafs star Darryl Sittler during an 11–4 victory over the Boston Bruins on February 7, 1976. That night Sittler would fire six goals and add four assists to set a new NHL record with a 10-point game.

11 With this stick Wayne Gretzky scored his 92nd and final goal of the 1981–82 NHL season, surpassing Phil Esposito's single-season record of 76 goals. Gretzky's record still stands as the NHL's highest single-season total.

12 Phil Esposito of the New York Rangers became the second player in NHL history to record 650 career markers after scoring the game-winning goal with this stick in a 4–2 victory over the Detroit Red Wings on December 27, 1978.

13 Stick used by Adam Oates on January 14, 2002, to collect the 1,000th assist of his illustrious career, becoming just the eighth NHL player to reach that milestone.

Page 120

1 Delaney Collins of the Calgary Oval X-Treme used this stick in the 2007 Esso Women's Nationals gold-medal game to record a goal and an assist in Calgary's 3–0 defeat of the Etobicoke Dolphins.

2 Stick used by Vicki Movsessian-Lamoriello of Team USA at the 1998 Olympics. She helped the Americans capture the first-ever women's hockey Olympic gold medal.

3 Cecilia Ostberg used this stick while representing Sweden in 2008 at the inaugural IIHF World Women's Under-18 Championship. Sweden finished fourth.

4 Laura Hurd of the Elmira College Soaring Eagles used this stick to score the championship-winning goal at the 2002 NCAA Division III finals.

5 Stick used by Canada's Hayley Wickenheiser to help Canada win the 4 Nations Cup in 2002. She was named tournament MVP.

6 Stick used by Jayna Hefford of Team Canada during the gold-medal game of the 2000 Women's World Championship, where she registered two third-period goals, forcing the game to overtime and helping Canada capture its sixth straight title.

7 Stacey Wilson, then captain of Team Canada, used this stick in the gold-medal game of the 1998 Winter Olympics, a 3–2 loss to the U.S.

8 Geraldine Heaney of the Toronto Aeros used this stick to score the overtime gold-medal-winning goal at the 2004 Esso Women's Nationals.

9 Sweden's Maria Rooth used this stick to score the only goal in a tight contest against Finland for the bronze medal at the 2007 Women's World Championship.

10 Jennifer Botterill scored the gold-medal-winning goal of the 2005 Esso Women's Nationals with this stick, as her Toronto Aeros won their second straight title.

11 Stick used by Danielle Bourgeois of the University of Alberta Pandas to score the championship-winning goal at the 2004 Canadian Interuniversity Sport women's final.

12 Tricia Guest of the University of Minnesota-Duluth Bulldogs used this stick to score the championship-winning goal at the 2002 NCAA Division I final.

13 Stick used by Ylva Viktoria Nordli of Team Norway during the 2003 Women's World Championship Division II tournament, where Norway won gold.

14 Robin Marvin of the Minnesota Blue J's used this stick to score the championship-winning goal at the 2000 U.S. Women's Senior AAA final.

15 Caroline Ouellette of Canada used this stick to lead the Canadians to a gold-medal victory over Sweden at the 2006 Olympics.

16 Krissy Wendell used this stick to help the Americans finish second at the 2007 Women's World Championship, where she finished second in tournament scoring.

17 Stick used by Pernilla Winberg of Sweden during the semifinals at the 2006 Olympics to score the only goal in the first-ever women's Olympic hockey shoot-out. Winberg's goal sent Sweden to their first-ever Olympic gold-medal game.

Page 121

1. One-piece wooden stick used by "Cyclone" Taylor during his one season as an Ottawa Senator, 1908–09. The stick is carved with the names of Cyclone's teammates.

2. Stick used by Paul Polillo of the Port Huron Border Cats to record his 1,000th UHL career point, an assist, on February 14, 1999, versus the Muskegon Fury.

3. On February 14, 1977, rookie defenseman Al Hill of the Philadelphia Flyers scored with this stick on his first shot. It came 36 seconds into the game, the second-fastest first goal in NHL history. By game's end he had set the record for points in a first NHL game, with five.

4. Charlie Conacher scored his final NHL career goal (225) with this stick during the 1940–41 season as a member of the New York Americans.

5. Stick used by Reginald "Hooley" Smith during the 1934–35 NHL season as a member of the Montreal Maroons team that defeated Chicago, New York and Toronto en route to the club's second Stanley Cup.

6. Montreal's Henri Richard scored his 200th NHL career goal with this stick on November 28, 1964, versus the Boston Bruins.

7. Stick used by Chicago's Marian Hossa during the Blackhawks' Game 6 2010 Stanley Cup victory. Hossa became the first player to play in three consecutive Cup finals with three different teams (the other two being Pittsburgh and Detroit).

8. Yvan Cournoyer of the Montreal Canadiens used this stick to record the 250th goal of his career on November 18, 1972.

9. Edmonton's Mark Messier used this stick to beat LA Kings netminder Mario Lessard for his 50th goal of the 1981–82 season, making Messier the fifth-youngest player in NHL history to reach that milestone.

10. Stick used by Ron Francis of the Pittsburgh Penguins to beat Quebec netminder Jocelyn Thibault on October 28, 1993. The goal was the 1,000th point of Francis' career.

11. Stick used by Detroit's Brendan Shanahan during Game 5 of the 2002 Stanley Cup final, when he potted two goals for the Wings in a 3–1 victory, including the all-important Cup winner at 14:04 of the second period.

12. Toronto captain Syl Apps used this stick during the final regular season game of his 10-year NHL career, on March 21, 1948, at the Olympia in Detroit. He recorded a hat trick and moved his all-time goal total to 201.

13. Stick used by Tim Horton during Game 7 of the 1964 Stanley Cup final versus the Detroit Red Wings. The Leafs would blank the Wings 4–0 on home ice to capture their third consecutive Stanley Cup title.

14. Gordie Roberts of the Boston Bruins was using this stick when he became the first U.S.-born player to play 1,000 games, on December 9, 1992.

15. Stick used by Willie O'Ree of the Boston Bruins during his only full season in the NHL, 1960–61. O'Ree became the first African-American player to participate in the NHL, breaking hockey's color barrier by playing two games for the Bruins in the 1957–58 season.

16. Stick used by Angela James of the North York Beatrice Aeros to score her final career goal during her final game, a National Women's Hockey League matchup versus the Laval Mistral on December 10, 2000.

17. Montreal's Steve Shutt used this stick to record his 400th career goal in a game against New Jersey on December 20, 1983, the same night teammate Guy Lafleur scored his 500th career goal.

18. Team USA forward Dave Christian used this stick during the 1980 Lake Placid Olympics, leading his team to a 4–3 upset of the Soviets on the way to a gold-medal victory over Finland.

19. Stick used by Joe Mullen of the Pittsburgh Penguins to record his 1,000th career point, an assist in his 935th career game, on February 7, 1995. Mullen's assist made him the first U.S.-born NHLer to reach that mark.

20. One of 51 sticks used by Wayne Gretzky during his final NHL game, on April 18, 1999. Gretzky used one stick per shift, giving one to each of his teammates and coaches following the game. With this stick Gretzky recorded a second assist on a Brian Leetch goal, his final NHL point – number 2,857.

21. On January 14, 1988, New York Islanders defenseman Denis Potvin made history with this stick, becoming the first defenseman to score 300 NHL career goals.

22. Stick used by Washington Capitals sniper Mike Gartner to record the only 50-goal season of his career, on April 7, 1985, during the Caps' final game of the regular season.

Page 125

1   Puck used to score the championship-winning goal for Hungary while they were hosting the 1998 C Pool World Championship; a 3–2 win over Romania gave Hungary its first-ever World Senior Championship gold medal.

2   Detroit's Modere "Mud" Bruneteau scored the overtime winner, and only goal of the game, versus the Montreal Maroons during Game 1 of their 1936 semifinal series with this puck. It was the NHL's longest game, clocking in at 116 minutes, 30 seconds.

3   Alexander Mogilny of the Buffalo Sabres used this puck to become the first Soviet-born player to record a 50-goal season when he scored on Hartford netminder Sean Burke on February 3, 1993.

4   Pat LaFontaine of the Verdun Junior Canadiens used this puck to record his 99th goal of the 1982–83 QMJHL season. The American smashed numerous rookie-scoring records and was named the CHL's Player of the Year.

5   Randy Murphy of the New Mexico Scorpions scored with this puck at 19:56 of the third period during a 5–3 WPHL victory over El Paso on December 31, 1999. That goal, scored in Albuquerque, New Mexico, was the final pro hockey goal scored during the 20th century and the millennium, coming at 9:59:56 p.m. mountain standard time.

6   Belarus' Ruslan Salei became the first active NHLer to score a goal at any Olympics when he scored with this puck in an 8–2 victory over Germany at the 1998 Winter Olympics, the NHL's first participation at the Games.

7   Gordie Howe of the Detroit Red Wings became the first player to reach 700 goals when he scored on Les Binkley of the Pittsburgh Penguins on December 9, 1968. This puck, long believed to be the actual goal puck, was used in now-famous photos after the game.

8   Puck used by Quebec Remparts' Mario Marois to score the first goal of his QMJHL career, during an October 31, 1975, game versus the Sorel Black Hawks. Marois would finish the season with 53 points.

9   Late in the 1970–71 season, Chicago's Bobby Hull used this puck to score his 545th NHL career goal, becoming the second player (and the first of three players in the 1970s) to surpass Maurice Richard's goal-scoring benchmark.

Page 127

1   Team Sweden superstar Maria Rooth fired this puck past Kazak netminder Darya Obydennova during a round-robin game at the 2009 Women's World Championship to record the 100th goal of her national team career.

2   Joe Sakic fired this puck through a crowd, off U.S. defenseman Brian Leetch and past goaltender Mike Richter to give Canada a 3–2 lead in the men's gold-medal final at the 2002 Olympics. The goal proved to be the winner, and Canada claimed the gold over the U.S. with a 5–2 victory.

3   Rhett Gordon of the Canadian National Team scored the game-winning goal over the Ontario University Athletics Select team with this puck on January 11, 2000. The national team was disbanded following that season.

4   New York Rangers center Marcel Dionne fired this puck past New York Islanders goaltender Kelly Hrudey to become just the third NHL player to reach the 700-career-goal milestone on October 31, 1987.

5   Puck used by Maurice "Rocket" Richard on October 19, 1957, to beat Chicago's Glenn Hall for the 500th goal of his career, making him the first player in NHL history to reach that milestone.

6   Puck used by LA's Wayne Gretzky to score the first of his two goals when he traded teams and suited up for the IHL's Phoenix Roadrunners during a September 26, 1993, exhibition game.

7   Don Parsons of the Central Hockey League's Quad City Mallards scored his 622nd goal with this puck on March 21, 2007. The goal tied him with legendary NHL sniper Joe Mullen for the most career goals scored by an American for all combined levels of professional hockey.

8   Puck used by Mike Richard of the Binghamton Whalers on December 23, 1987, to record a point in his 31st consecutive AHL game, setting a new league record for consecutive games with a goal.

9   Slovakia's Peter Bondra used this puck to score the championship-winning goal at the 2002 World Championship, earning Slovakia its first world title.

stall 1   stall 2   stall 3   stall 4

Pages 146–147

STALL 1 (BURE)

(*Skates*) Washington's Jaromir Jagr wore these skates on February 4, 2003, when he recorded a hat trick against the Tampa Bay Lightning. The third goal of the trick was his 500th career goal.

(*Gloves*) Gloves worn by Vincent Damphousse of the San Jose Sharks on October 14, 2000, when he assisted on a Marco Sturm goal for his 1,000th career point.

(*Jersey*) Vancouver's Pavel Bure wore this jersey for the 1992–93 season, during which he led the Canucks in points, with a career-high 110.

(*Pants*) Pants worn by Dallas' Joe Nieuwendyk during the 1999 Stanley Cup final versus the Buffalo Sabres. Nieuwendyk won the Conn Smythe Trophy and tied a playoff record with six game-winning goals.

(*Helmet*) Colorado Avalanche center Pierre Turgeon wore this helmet on November 8, 2005, when he scored his 500th career goal in a 5–3 win over the San Jose Sharks.

(*Socks*) Nicklas Lidstrom, captain of the Detroit Red Wings, wore these socks in 2008 while leading the franchise to its 11th Stanley Cup victory, making him the first European captain to be presented the Stanley Cup.

STALL 2 (NO.10)

(*Skates*) Skates worn by New York Islanders star Pat LaFontaine during the 1987–88 NHL season. LaFontaine led the Islanders in goals (47) and points (92).

(*Gloves*) Carolina's Cory Stillman wore these gloves during the 2006 Stanley Cup final, during which he finished second in playoff scoring with 26 points, including an assist on the Cup-winning goal.

(*Helmet*) Helmet worn by Tampa Bay Lightning forward Martin St. Louis during the 2003–04 season, when he led the league in scoring, was named league MVP and helped the Lightning win the Stanley Cup.

(*Jersey*) Jersey worn by Alex Delvecchio during a portion of his 24 years with the Detroit Red Wings, during which he recorded 456 goals and 1,281 points and was a three-time winner of the Lady Byng Trophy.

(*Pants*) Detroit's Steve Yzerman wore these pants for his final NHL season, in 2005–06. Yzerman retired with 1,755 points, the sixth-highest all-time NHL total.

(*Shoulder pads*) Rob Niedermayer of the Anaheim Ducks wore these shoulder pads for the 2006–07 NHL season, when he helped the Ducks vanquish the Ottawa Senators in five games for the Stanley Cup.

STALL 3 (GILMOUR)

(*Skates*) Skates worn by Sidney Crosby of the Pittsburgh Penguins for the first four games of the 2007–08 NHL season, before he suffered an ankle injury that limited him to 53 games.

(*Gloves*) Craig Muni of the Buffalo Sabres wore these gloves during the 1994–95 NHL season, his only season with Buffalo.

(*Helmet*) Anders Hedberg of the New York Rangers wore this helmet during the late 1970s and early 80s. Hedberg was one of the NHL's first foreign stars, after having spent four years in the WHA.

(*Jersey*) Toronto Maple Leafs jersey worn by captain Doug Gilmour during the 1992–93 NHL season. Gilmour had a career-best season, setting Maple Leaf single-season records for assists (95) and points (127).

(*Shoulder pads*) Detroit's Steve Yzerman wore these shoulder pads for his final NHL season, in 2005–06. Yzerman retired as Detroit's all-time playoff leader in goals (70), assists (115) and points (185).

(*Pants*) Jordan Staal of the Pittsburgh Penguins wore these pants during his rookie year; he was named to the 2006–07 NHL All-Rookie Team.

(*Socks*) Socks worn by Toronto's Pavel Kubina for the Ninth Annual HHOF Game on November 8, 2008. The Leafs defenseman registered one goal and one assist to earn Player of the Game honors.

STALL 4 (HAWERCHUK)

(*Skates*) Mike Gartner of the New York Rangers wore these skates for the 1992–93 season, his 14th consecutive 30-plus goal season.

(*Gloves*) Gloves worn by Washington's Rod Langway during the early 1990s. Langway spent 11 of his 15 NHL seasons with the Capitals, all as team captain, and won the Norris Trophy twice (1983 and 1984).

(*Helmet*) Pittsburgh's Mark Recchi wore this helmet during a January 26, 2007, game in Dallas, Texas, where he scored the 500th goal of his NHL career.

(*Jersey*) Dale Hawerchuk, 1981–82 Rookie of the Year, wore this Winnipeg Jets jersey during his mid-1980s NHL action. Hawerchuk played nine seasons with the Jets, recording six 100-plus-point campaigns.

(*Shoulder pads*) New Jersey's Scott Niedermayer wore these shoulder pads for the 2000 playoffs. Niedermayer scored a shorthanded goal in Game 6 of the final versus Dallas, as the Devils captured the Stanley Cup with a 2–1 victory.

(*Pants*) Washington Capitals pants worn by Dino Ciccarelli for the 1990–91 NHL season, his first full season in Washington after being traded by Minnesota.

(*Socks*) New Jersey Devils defenseman Ken Daneyko wore these socks during his final NHL playoff run in 2003, helping the club capture its third Stanley Cup title.

Page 147

STALL 5 (NO. 5)

(*Skates*) Skates Frank Foyston wore during the latter portion of his 18-year professional hockey career. Foyston would win three Stanley Cups: 1914, with Toronto; 1917, with Seattle; and 1925, with Victoria.

(*Gloves*) Gloves worn by Neil Colville of the New York Rangers during his early 1940s NHL action. Colville spent three stints with the Rangers between 1935 and 1949; his breaks were due to time spent in the armed forces during World War II.

(*Helmet*) Murray Craven wore this helmet during a portion of his seven complete seasons with the Philadelphia Flyers, helping them reach the Stanley Cup final in both 1984 and 1987.

(*Sweater*) Aubrey "Dit" Clapper wore this sweater during one of his 20 NHL seasons with the Boston Bruins. Clapper was a six-time All-Star and led the Bruins to three Stanley Cup championships.

(*Shoulder pads*) Shoulder pads worn by Scott Stevens throughout his 22-year NHL career, which saw him play for Washington, St. Louis and New Jersey and win three Stanley Cups with the Devils, as well as the Conn Smythe Trophy in 2000.

(*Pants*) New Jersey's Ken Daneyko wore these pants during the 2000 playoffs. The Devils defeated the Dallas Stars to win their second Stanley Cup.

STALL 6 (LOPRESTI)

(*Skates*) Jean-Sébastien Giguère wore these skates while leading the Anaheim Ducks to their first Stanley Cup title, in 2007. He posted a 1.97 playoff goals-against average.

(*Gloves*) Tomas Vokoun of the Florida Panthers wore these gloves during the 2008–09 season. Vokoun faced the most shots in the league (2,213) and made the most saves (2,033).

(*Jersey*) Minnesota North Stars jersey worn by Gump Worsley during his final NHL career season, 1973–74. The jersey was then re-stitched with a new name and worn the following season by rookie Pete Lopresti.

(*Pants*) Pants worn by Jacques Cloutier during his final season as a member of the Buffalo Sabres, in 1988–89. After seven seasons as a Sabre, Cloutier was moved to the Chicago Blackhawks.

(*Helmet*) Mike Richter of the New York Rangers wore this mask during the second half of the 1996–97 NHL season, during which he compiled 33 regular season wins. He was coming off an MVP performance at the 1996 World Cup of Hockey.

(*Pads*) Billy Smith of the New York Islanders wore these signature two-tone Koho pads during the early- to mid-1980s. Smith won four consecutive Stanley Cups (1980 to 1983) with the Islanders and was presented the Vezina Trophy in 1982.

Page 152

1 EDINBURGH TROPHY: Awarded to the champion of a challenge series between the winner of the Western Hockey League and the Quebec Hockey League. The trophy was only contested from 1953–54 to 1956–57.

2 JACK ADAMS CUP: Awarded to the playoff champion of the Central Professional Hockey League from 1963–64 until the league's demise in 1983–84. The trophy is named after Jack Adams, Hockey Hall of Fame player, legendary Detroit Red Wings general manager and founding president of the CPHL.

3 LESTER PATRICK CUP: Awarded to the playoff champion of the professional Western Hockey League from 1952–53 until the league's demise in 1973–74. Originally the WHL playoff champions were given the Phil Henderson Cup, which was replaced by the President's Cup for the 1952–53 championship. The President's Cup was renamed in 1960–61 to honor the late Lester Patrick, an early West Coast hockey pioneer and builder of the Pacific Coast Hockey League, the forerunner to the WHL.

4 AVCO WORLD TROPHY: World Hockey Association playoff championship trophy. It was donated to the new league in 1972 along with approximately $500,000 by the AVCO Financial Services Corporation, making the WHA the only major sports league at the time to have its championship prize hold the name of a private corporation.

5 JOSEPH TURNER MEMORIAL CUP: Awarded to the playoff champion of the International Hockey League from 1945–46 until the league's demise in 2000–01. The award is named after Joe Turner, a Windsor, Ontario, goalie who played in the Michigan-Ontario Hockey League and turned pro with the Detroit Red Wings. He played with Detroit's American Hockey League farm club, the Indianapolis Capitols, leading them to the AHL championship in 1942. Turner was killed in action in World War II on December 13, 1944, as a member of the United States Army.

Page 153

1. The Allan Cup was donated by Sir H. Montague Allan, C.V.O., shortly after the Stanley Cup became the championship trophy of professional hockey and was originally a challenge trophy open to any senior amateur club having won the championship of its league that year. It was first awarded in 1909 to the Ottawa Cliffsides. In 1914 the Allan Cup became the award for the best amateur team of the newly formed Canadian Hockey Association. In 1984, the classification changed again, and the Allan Cup has since been awarded annually to the best Senior AAA club in Canada.

2. The George Taylor Richardson Memorial Trophy was named in honor of Hockey Hall of Fame member George Richardson, who died in World War I. The trophy was awarded to the junior hockey champion of eastern Canada from 1932 to 1971.

3. Championship bowl donated by the Montreal Arena Company to the Eastern Canadian Amateur Hockey Association to be used as its championship prize. The league lasted four years, 1906–09.

4. The Boardwalk Cup originated as a prize for the 1932 Amateur Athletic Union hockey champion, and it eventually became the Eastern Hockey League playoff championship trophy. It was awarded until the league disbanded in 1973.

5. The championship cup from the Oxford–Cambridge Challenge Shield hockey game played by age-old rivals Cambridge and Oxford on a lake in the Swiss Alps in 1910. The first varsity match between the two clubs took place in 1885, and the Oxford–Cambridge match is the oldest ongoing hockey rivalry in the world.

6. The Canadian Amateur Hockey League Trophy was awarded to the regular-season winner of the CAHL from 1898–99 to 1904–05. In December 1905 the CAHL merged with the rival Federal Amateur Hockey League.

7. First awarded in 1891, the Senior Championship Trophy (considered the forerunner to the Stanley Cup) was awarded to the champions of the Amateur Hockey Association and in its day was the premier hockey trophy in Canada. The trophy bears an inscription stating that if any team should ever win it three times, it would become the property of that team. The Montreal Wanderers won the 1891 championship and defended their title twice more in succession, thus winning the trophy three times and thereby retiring it from competition. It was at this time that Lord Stanley donated his Dominion Challenge Cup, more commonly known as the Stanley Cup.

Page 154

1. A championship medallion from the British Ice Hockey Association's 1952 Winston Churchill Cup that was presented to English Selects coach Frank Boucher. Boucher led the Selects (a team made up of members from the Wembley Lions, Earls Court Rangers and Harringay Racers) to a 6–4 victory over Canada's Edmonton Mercurys to claim the championship.

2. Participation medal awarded to Team Great Britain goaltender Charles Little at the 1931 World Championship, held in Krynica, Poland.

3. Medallion presented to Ottawa 67's head coach Brian Kilrea following the club's first Ontario Major Junior Hockey League championship, in 1976–77.

4. Gold medal presented to Team Canada coach Pat Quinn by the IIHF after Canada's gold-medal victory at the 2002 Olympics. Coaches are not awarded Olympic medals, making this award very unique.

5. Jayna Hefford's 2004 Women's World Championship gold medal. Hefford led all players at the tournament with seven goals and earned top tournament forward honors.

6. Platter awarded to Tommy Ivan, head coach of the 1949–50 Stanley Cup–champion Detroit Red Wings.

Page 164

The Memorial Cup was donated by the Ontario Hockey Association in March 1919 in remembrance of the many young men and women who lost their lives for Canada in World War I. Initially the Memorial Cup was awarded to the national junior hockey champions of Canada. Today the champions of the Western Hockey League (WHL), the Quebec Major Junior Hockey League (QMJHL) and the Ontario Hockey League (OHL) and a host club meet each spring in a round-robin series, with the two top teams playing each other in a sudden-death game to determine the Memorial Cup champion.

Page 171

1   The Coupe Purolator, awarded from 1986 to 1988, was the championship prize for Hockey Quebec's province-wide minor hockey tournament. Today the tournament is called the Coupe Dodge.

2   The Upper Deck NHL All-Rookie Team Trophy was awarded to the team selected by the Professional Hockey Writers' Association as the most proficient at their respective positions in their first NHL season. The physical trophy was awarded from 1990 to 1993.

3   The Budweiser NHL Man of the Year Trophy was awarded between 1987–88 and 1991–92. It recognized players for their community-building initiatives. Players in the NHL are now recognized with the Foundation Player Award for their community initiatives.

4   The Shipstads and Johnson Perpetual Challenge Trophy was awarded to the Northern Division champs of the Pacific Coast Hockey League. The PCHL ran from 1944–45 to 1951–52 and was a precursor to the Western Hockey League. Shipstads and Johnson were the men who created the live ice show Ice Follies.

Page 172

1 TED LINDSAY AWARD: The National Hockey League Players' Association has voted a "most outstanding player" since 1970–71. This distinction was marked with the presentation of the Lester B. Pearson Award, in honor of the Canadian Prime Minister from 1963 to 1967. Carrying on the tradition established by the Pearson Award, the Ted Lindsay Award was created in 2010. The award is named in honor of Hall of Famer Ted Lindsay for his role in establishing the original Players' Association. All Pearson Award winners are recognized together on the Ted Lindsay Award.

2 MAURICE RICHARD TROPHY: This trophy is presented to the league's leading goal-scorer and was donated by the Montreal Canadiens in 1999 to honor Maurice Richard. Richard was the first player to have a 50-goal season and was the league's top goal-scorer five times.

3 CALDER MEMORIAL TROPHY: The NHL first announced a Rookie of the Year in 1933, but it wasn't until the 1936–37 season that a trophy was awarded. The trophy was named the Calder Trophy, after then-president Frank Calder. After Calder's sudden death in 1943, the award became known as the Calder Memorial Trophy. The winner is selected by polling the Professional Hockey Writers' Association.

4 JACK ADAMS AWARD: Though inducted into the Hockey Hall of Fame as a player, Jack Adams is best remembered as the Detroit Red Wings' coach during the 1940s and 1950s. In 1974 the NHL Broadcasters' Association created this award in his honor. It is given to the NHL coach judged to have contributed the most to his team's success during the season. The winner is voted by the NHL Broadcasters' Association.

5 CLARENCE S. CAMPBELL BOWL: Introduced by the NHL in 1968 in recognition of the services of Clarence S. Campbell, president of the NHL from 1946 to 1977, the Bowl was originally presented to the regular-season champions of the West Division. Beginning in 1975 it was awarded to the regular-season champion of the Campbell Conference, and from 1982 to 1993 the Bowl was awarded to the Campbell Conference playoff champion. Since 1993–94 the trophy has been presented to the playoff champion of the Western Conference.

6 BILL MASTERTON MEMORIAL TROPHY: Bill Masterton, an All-American and MVP of the 1961 NCAA tournament, retired from professional hockey in 1964, having played in the minors his entire career. In 1967, while a member of the U.S. National Team, Masterton's rights were bought by the expansion Minnesota North Stars. Only 38 games into his first NHL season, Masterton was bodychecked unconscious. He never woke from his coma and died two days later, on January 15, 1968. The NHL introduced this trophy in his honor at the end of the 1967–68 season. It is awarded to the player who best exhibits the dedication and sportsmanship Masterton embodied. Voting is conducted by the Professional Hockey Writers' Association.

7 ART ROSS TROPHY: In 1947 Art Ross, the legendary Boston Bruins executive, donated a trophy to the NHL. It is awarded to the player who scores the most points during the regular season.

8 WILLIAM M. JENNINGS TROPHY: This trophy was introduced during the 1981–82 season in honor of William M. Jennings, longtime governor and owner of the New York Rangers. It replaced the Vezina Trophy as the prize for the goaltender(s) of the team allowing the fewest number of goals during the regular season.

9 KING CLANCY MEMORIAL TROPHY: It was introduced in 1988 in honor of the late King Clancy, who was a player, official, coach and executive. The trophy is awarded to the player who best exemplifies leadership, on and off the ice, and who has made notable humanitarian contributions. The winner is selected by polling the Professional Hockey Writers' Association.

Page 173

1 PRESIDENTS' TROPHY: Presented to the NHL by the board of governors for the 1985–86 season, the Presidents' Trophy is awarded annually to the team with the best regular-season record. In the case of a tie, the trophy goes to the team with the most wins.

2 VEZINA TROPHY: In 1926–27, Léo Dandurand, Louis Létourneau and Joe Cattarinich, former owners of the Montreal Canadiens, donated a trophy in memory of Habs goaltender Georges Vezina. It was awarded to the goaltender(s) of the team allowing the fewest number of goals during the regular season. The trophy's definition changed in 1981–82, with the prize being awarded to the NHL's best overall goaltender as voted by the league's GMs.

3 PRINCE OF WALES TROPHY: The Prince of Wales donated this trophy to the NHL in 1924. From 1927–28 through 1937–38 the award was presented to the winner of the American Division. From 1938–39 to 1966–67 the team with the best regular-season record claimed the trophy. With expansion in 1967–68, the trophy was awarded to the regular-season East Division champion. Beginning in 1974–75, the regular-season winner of the Prince of Wales Conference claimed the trophy, and from 1981–82 to 1992–93 the playoff champion of the Wales Conference was presented the hardware. Since 1993–94, the trophy has been presented to the playoff champion of the Eastern Conference.

4 STANLEY CUP: The Stanley Cup is the oldest trophy awarded to professional athletes in North America. The Cup was donated by Lord Stanley of Preston in 1892 to be awarded to "the championship hockey club of the Dominion of Canada." The National Hockey Association took possession of the Stanley Cup in 1910, and it has been awarded to NHL teams exclusively since 1927.

5 JAMES NORRIS MEMORIAL TROPHY: First awarded in 1954, this trophy was named after long-time Detroit Red Wings owner James Norris, whose family controlled the Wings from 1932 to 1982. Every year it is presented to the defenseman who demonstrates the greatest all-around ability in his position. The winner is selected by polling the Professional Hockey Writers' Association.

6 FRANK J. SELKE TROPHY: The Selke Trophy was introduced in 1977 to recognize the top defensive forward in the league. The trophy was named after Frank J. Selke, a former executive with both the Toronto Maple Leafs and the Montreal Canadiens who was instrumental in building Maple Leaf Gardens. The winner is selected by polling the Professional Hockey Writers' Association.

7 CONN SMYTHE TROPHY: In 1964 Maple Leaf Gardens donated a trophy in honor of Conn Smythe, former coach, general manager and owner of the Toronto Maple Leafs. It is awarded to the most valuable player of the playoffs, regardless of whether that player is on the winning or loosing squad. Voting is conducted by the Professional Hockey Writers' Association.

8 HART MEMORIAL TROPHY: One of the NHL's longest-standing prizes, the Hart Trophy was donated in 1923 by Dr. David Hart, father of Montreal Canadiens coach Cecil Hart. The trophy is presented to the most valuable player of the regular season. Voting is conducted by the Professional Hockey Writers' Association.

9 LADY BYNG MEMORIAL TROPHY: Lady Byng, wife of Canada's then–governor general, the Viscount Byng, donated a trophy in 1925 to be awarded to the player who exhibits the most gentlemanly conduct and sportsmanship combined with excellent skill. Frank Boucher of the New York Rangers won the award seven times in eight seasons, and he was given the original trophy. Lady Byng donated a second trophy in 1936. After her death in 1949, the NHL presented a third trophy, the Lady Byng Memorial Trophy. Voting is conducted by the Professional Hockey Writers' Association.

INDEX

3 Nations Cup: 56–57
4 Nations Cup: 212
24/7 Penguins/Capitals: Road to the NHL Winter Classic: 188
"200 Club": 184
1972 Summit Series: 45, 71, 106, 118–119, 132, 133, 192–193, 212
1974 Summit Series: 45, 206

Adams, Jack: 159, 216, 219
Adams, Kevyn: 158–159
AHL see American Hockey League
Air Canada Centre: 192–193
Ak Bars Kazan: 111
Alexandria Glens: 209
All-Americans: 99, 141, 219 see also NCAA
Allan Cup: 9, 153, 206, 217
Allan, Sir H. Montague, C.V.O.: 217
Allen, Harry: 46, 206
All-Rookie Team, NHL: 215
All-Star Games, AHL: 140
All-Star Games, ECHL: 106
All-Star Games, NHL: 104, 139, 196, 201, 202, 208, 209
All-Stars, NHL: 69, 92, 166, 196, 209, 210, 216
Amateur Athletic Union: 217
Amateur Hockey Association: 217
American Division: 220
American Hockey League (AHL): 99, 140, 155, 207, 214, 216
Anaheim Ducks: 85, 115, 156–157, 209, 215, 216
Anaheim Mighty Ducks see Anaheim Ducks
Anderson, Glenn: 58–59, 207
Anderson, Lorne: 55
Andersson, Gunilla: 211
Andress, Brenda: 161
Andreychuk, Dave: 68, 85, 209
Apps, Syl: 121, 213
Arkansas River Blades: 106
Armstrong, Neil: 48–49
Art Ross Trophy: 70, 172, 219
Atlanta Flames: 27, 102, 208, 210
Atlanta Thrashers: 208
Atlantic Division, NHL: 210
Australian National Team: 43
Austrian Hockey League: 83
Avalanche see Colorado Avalanche
AVCO World Trophy: 152, 216

Bailey, Ace: 65, 104, 208
Bain, Dan: 182
Baker, Hobey: 202
Baker, Thornton: 202
Ballard, Harold: 196
Bannerman, Murray: 102
Barber, Bill: 201
Barilko, Bill: 65, 122–123, 124, 208

Barlow, Billy: 156–157
Barons see Cleveland Barons
Barrasso, Tom: 99
Barry, Marty "Goal-a-game": 201
Bathgate, Andy: 58–59, 88, 207
Bauer, Father David: 159
Bechard, Kelly: 58–59, 207
Bélanger, Yves: 102
Belarusan National Team: 214
Belfour, Ed: 91, 102
Béliveau, Jean: 28, 52, 53, 65, 206, 208
Bentley, Doug: 85, 142
Berenson, Gordon "Red": 141
Berg, Aki-Petteri: 108, 211
Bidini, Dave: 13, 21–22, 25, 111–112, 115
Bill Masterton Memorial Trophy: 172, 219
Bilyaletdinov, Diniyar: 111
Binghamton Whalers: 214
Binkley, Les: 214
Blachford, Cecil: 142
Black Hawks see Chicago Blackhawks
Blackhawks see Chicago Blackhawks
Black, Joe: 184
Blake, Toe: 86
Blinov, Yuri: 21
Blues see St. Louis Blues
Boardwalk Cup: 153, 217
Bodnar, Gus: 55
Bondra, Peter: 127, 214
Boon, Dickie: 83
Bossy, Mike: 58–59, 63, 64, 65, 170, 207, 208
Boston Bruins: 36–37, 41, 50–51, 95, 104, 106, 107, 142, 143, 207, 208, 212, 213, 216, 219
Boston College Eagles: 207
Boston Garden: 104
Boston University: 106
Botterill, Jennifer: 120, 212
Boucher, Brian: 60–61, 99, 207
Boucher, Frank: 154, 217, 220
Bourgeois, Danielle: 120, 212
Bower, Johnny: 96
Bowman, Scotty: 8–9
Brampton Thunder: 207
Bretto, Joe: 140
British Columbia Hockey League: 207
British Ice Hockey Association: 217
Broten, Neal: 209
Bruins see Boston Bruins
Bruneteau, Modere "Mud": 125, 214
Bubla, Jiri: 22
Bucyk, John: 58–59, 193, 207
Budweiser NHL Man of the Year Trophy: 171, 218

Buffalo Bisons: 99
Buffalo Sabres: 27, 85, 99, 112, 207, 208, 209, 214, 215, 216
Bure, Pavel: 146, 215
Burke, Sean: 214
Bylsma, Dan: 204
Byng, Lady: 220

Calder Cup: 140, 155, 207
Calder, Frank: 219
Calder Memorial Trophy: 172, 219
Calder Trophy: 219
Calgary Flames: 48–49, 145 156, 202, 206, 208, 209
Calgary Oval X-Treme: 207, 212
California Golden Seals: 83, 139, 212
Cambridge University: 217
Campbell, Cassie: 162
Campbell, Clarence: 11, 48–49, 219
Campbell Conference, NHL: 139, 219
Campbell, Craig: 201, 204
Canada Cup: 43, 131, 166–167, 206
Canadian Amateur Hockey League: 217
Canadian Amateur Hockey League Trophy: 153, 217
Canadian Hockey Association: 217
Canadian Interuniversity Sport: 206, 210, 212
Canadian National Junior Team: 56–57, 115, 168, 207
Canadian National Team: 9, 25, 36, 44–45, 46–47, 56–57, 71, 74, 96, 128, 130–131, 132, 159, 166, 185, 188, 200, 206, 207, 208, 210, 211, 212, 214, 217
Canadian National Team program: 159
Canadian National Women's Team: 56–57, 74, 96, 132, 162, 208, 211, 212
Canadian Women's Hockey League: 162
Canadiens see Montreal Canadiens
Canucks see Vancouver Canucks
Cariboo Hockey League: 203
Carlson, Jack: 136–137
Carolina Hurricanes: 116, 159, 201, 202, 215
Carpenter, Bobby: 64, 208
Carson, Jimmy: 64, 208
Casey, Jon: 102
Cattarinich, Joe: 220
Central Hockey League (CHL): 74, 79, 208, 214
Central Professional Hockey League (CPHL): 216
Chadwick, Ed: 99, 139
Chelios, Chris: 52, 206

Chicago Black Hawks see Chicago Blackhawks
Chicago Blackhawks: 26, 36, 48, 55, 56–57, 63, 72, 85, 102, 139, 142, 145, 156–157, 159, 187, 196, 207, 212, 213, 214, 216
Chicago Stadium: 49, 72, 190
Chicago Wolves: 207
CHL see Central Hockey League
Chouinard, Guy: 64, 208
Christian, Bill: 134–135
Christian, Dave: 121, 134–135, 213
Chubak, Carson: 60–61, 207
Ciccarelli, Dino: 147, 215
Cincinnati Stingers: 136–137
Civic Arena: 72
Clancy, King: 41, 219
Clapper, Aubrey "Dit": 147, 216
Clarence S. Campbell Bowl: 172, 219
Clark, Wendel: 20, 69, 209
Clarke, Bobby: 81, 141, 210
Clark, Maurice J.: 203
Clarkson, Adrienne: 160–163
Clarkson Cup: 160–163
Clarkson University Golden Knights: 141
Clark, Wendel: 20, 69, 209
Clemmensen, Scott: 60–61, 207
Cleveland Barons: 2, 4, 26
Cleveland Falcons: 140
Clinton Comets: 206
Cloutier, Jacques: 147, 216
Cloutier, Real: 28
Collins, Delaney: 120, 212
Colorado Avalanche: 92, 215
Colorado Eagles: 79
Colville, Neil: 147, 216
Conacher, Charlie: 121, 213
Canadian National Team see Canadian National Team
Conn Smythe Trophy: 82, 115, 173, 215, 216, 220
Conroy, Craig: 141
Copps Coliseum: 206
Coupe Dodge: 218
Coupe Purolator: 171, 218
Cournoyer, Yvan: 121, 213
Coyotes see Phoenix Coyotes
Craig, Jim: 91
Craven, Murray: 147, 216
Creston Jets: 209
Crosby, Sidney: 39, 128–129, 146, 185, 198, 208, 215
Crouch, Kim: 2, 4
CTV: 188
Czechoslovakian National Team: 206
Czech Republic National Team: 200, 208, 211

D'Alessandro, Mike: 97, 210
Dallas Stars: 74, 79, 85, 91, 116, 207, 215, 216
Damphousse, Vincent: 146, 215

Dandurand, Léo: 220
Daneyko, Ken: 114–115, 215, 216
Dannish National Team: 43
Davey, Gerry: 5
Davidson, Bob: 138–139
Delvecchio, Alex: 146, 215
Denomme, Jeff: 202
Denver Spurs: 136–137
Detroit Olympia: 72
Detroit Red Wings: 2, 4, 18, 19, 40–41, 56–57, 72, 73, 74, 76, 83, 90, 95, 156–157, 159, 206, 207, 208, 209, 212, 213, 214, 215, 216, 217, 219, 220
Devils see New Jersey Devils
Dewhurst, Robin: 43
Didier, Gord: 141
Die Adler Mannheim: 211
Dillabough, Bob: 65, 208
Dillon, Wayne: 136–137
Dionne, Marcel: 116–117, 127, 214
Djurgardens IF: 56–57
D.K. (Doc) Seaman Hockey Resource Centre: 198, 200, 201, 202, 203, 204
Dominion Challenge Cup: 149, 175, 217 see also Stanley Cup
Downie, Mike: 111
Drolet, Nancy: 109, 211
Ducks see Anaheim Ducks
Dumart, Woody: 143
Dunham, Mike: 97, 210
Durnan, Bill: 92–93
Dutch National Team see Netherlands National Team
Duthie, James: 185, 187–188

Earls Court Rangers: 217
East Division, NHL: 208, 220
Eastern Canadian Amateur Hockey Association: 217
Eastern Collegiate Hockey Association (ECHA): 142
Eastern Conference, NHL: 204, 210, 220
Eastern Hockey League: 206, 217
Eastern Ontario Junior B Hockey League: 209
EC Hedos Munchen: 27
ECHL: 74, 106, 136–137, 209
Edinburgh Trophy: 152, 193, 216
Edmonton Flyers: 192–193
Edmonton Mercurys: 46, 185, 188, 206, 217
Edmonton Oilers: 2, 4, 66, 91, 144–145, 207, 210, 213
EHC Kloten: 192–193
El Passo Buzzards: 76, 214
Elmer Ferguson Award: 189
Elmira College Soaring Eagles: 68, 209, 212

English Selects: 217
ESPN: 188
Esposito, Phil: 64, 114–115, 118–119, 208, 212
Esposito, Tony: 60–61, 187, 207
Essensa, Bob: 102
Etobicoke Dolphins: 212
EV Zug/Seewen: 211

Färjestad BK: 211
Federal Amateur Hockey League: 217
Federko, Bernie: 112–113
Ferguson, Elmer: 189
Fetisov, Viacheslav: 132
Finlay, Charles: 83
Finnish Ice Hockey Federation: 201
Finnish National Team: 56–57, 200, 207, 211, 213
Finnish National Women's League: 211
Finnish National Women's Team: 212
First All-Star Team: 92, 210 see also All-Stars, All-Star Games, Second All-Star Team
Flames see Calgary Flames
Fleury, Marc-André: 91, 97, 210
Fleury, Theoren: 47, 206
Flin Flon Bombers: 81, 141, 210
Flint Generals: 207
Florida Panthers: 112, 210, 216
Flyers see Philadelphia Flyers
Foote, Adam: 112–113
Forsberg, Peter: 108, 211
Fort McMurray Oil Barons: 56–57
Fort Wayne Komets: 79, 136
Foster Hewitt Award: 179
Foundation Player Award: 218
Founders' Room: 159
Foyston, Frank: 147, 216
Francis, Ron: 112–113, 114–115, 116–117, 121, 145, 213
Frank J. Selke Trophy: 173, 220
Friday, Bill: 48–49
Frozen Four Tournament: 99, 207
Ftorek, Robbie: 43
Fuhr, Grant: 2, 4, 116–117
Fumerton, Jet: 69, 209

Gajewski, Kyle: 60–61, 207
Gamble, Bruce: 53
Garrett, John: 2, 4
Gartner, Mike: 46, 71, 106, 118–119, 121, 147, 206, 212, 213, 215
Gaylord Entertainment Center: 210
Gehry, Frank: 166–167
George Taylor Richardson Memorial Trophy: 153, 217
German Ice Hockey League: 211
German National League: 211
German National Team: 214

Giacomin, Eddie: 90, 100
Giguère, Jean-Sébastien: 147, 216
Gilbert, Gilles: 208
Gillies, Clark: 114–115
Gillmor, Don: 73–74, 77
Gilmour, Doug: 146, 215
Goc, Sascha: 109, 211
"golden goal": 128–129, 208
Golden Seals see California Golden Seals
Goldup, Glenn: 71
Gordon, Rhett: 127, 214
Goulet, Michel: 52, 145, 206
Grahame, John: 63
Great Britain National Team: 5, 217
Green Bay Gamblers: 71
Gretzky, Walter: 77, 170
Gretzky, Wayne: 11, 20, 52, 63, 66–67, 79, 110, 112, 118–119, 121, 127, 144–145, 170, 177, 200, 206, 208, 212, 213, 214
Guest, Tricia: 120, 212

Habs see Montreal Canadiens
Hadfield, Vic: 64, 208
Haileybury Comets: 180–181
Hainsworth, George: 100
Hall, Glenn: 36–37, 127, 193, 196, 214
Hamburg Freezers: 211
Hamilton Bulldogs: 140
Hamilton Chewing Gum: 16
Hamilton Fincups: 141
Hanson, Dave: 136–137
Harbin, China: 21, 43
Harding, Josh: 60–61, 207
Harringay Racers: 217
Hart, Cecil: 220
Hart, David: 220
Hartford Whalers: 2, 4, 84, 115, 125, 145, 214
Hart, Gene: 184
Hart Memorial Trophy: 70, 173, 220
Hawerchuk, Dale: 147, 215
Hay, Bill: 156–157, 202
Haydar, Darren: 58–59, 207
Hayes, George: 48–49
Heaney, Geraldine: 120, 212
Heatley, Dany: 58–59, 207
Hedberg, Anders: 146, 215
Hefford, Jayna: 65, 109, 154, 208, 211, 212, 217
Hemsky, Ales: 109, 211
Henderson, Paul: 22, 118–119, 212
Hewitt, Foster: 10, 73, 179, 185
Hill, Al: 121, 213
Hirsch, Corey: 96
Hobey Baker Award: 202
Hockey Canada: 161
Hockey Hall of Fame Games: 192–193, 215
Hockey Night in Canada: 178–179, 184, 187
Hockey Quebec: 218

Hodge, Dave: 187
Hoganson, Paul: 136–137
Holik, Bobby: 116–117
Holmes, Harry "Hap": 60–61, 207
Holt, Greg: 52, 206
Horton, Tim: 121, 213
Hossa, Marian: 121, 213
Houston Aeros: 140
Howe, Gordie: 18, 19, 41, 65, 67, 70, 73, 83, 118–119, 125, 208, 212, 214
Hrudey, Kelly: 127, 214
Hull, Bobby: 8, 25, 30, 31, 46, 63, 65, 125, 206, 208, 214
Hull, Brett: 52, 63, 118–119, 145, 156, 206, 212
Hull Olympiques: 74
Hungarian league hockey: 43
Hungarian National Team: 211, 214
Huntsville Channel Cats: 74
Hurd, Laura: 68, 120, 209, 212
Hurricanes see Carolina Hurricanes

Iginla, Jarome: 65, 208
"Igloo": 72
IHL see International Hockey League
IIHF see International Ice Hockey Federation
Imlach, Punch: 24, 25, 77
Indianapolis Capitols: 216
International-American Hockey League (IAHL): 140
International Hockey League (IHL): 79, 136–137, 214, 216
International Ice Hockey Federation (IIHF): 43, 120, 132, 200, 217
International Olympic Committee (IOC): 32
Irbe, Arturs: 60–61, 207
Irvin, Dick: 184
Islanders see New York Islanders
Ivan, Tommy: 154, 159, 196, 217

Jack Adams Award: 172, 219
Jack Adams Cup: 152, 216
Jackson, Harvey "Busher": 142
Jackson, Paul: 64, 208
Jagr, Jaromir: 111, 146, 215
James, Angela: 121, 213
James Norris Memorial Trophy: 173, 220
Japanese National Team: 42–43
Jennings, William M.: 219
Jobe, Trevor: 69, 209
Joe Louis Arena: 72
Johannesson, Konrad: 132
Johnson, Bob: 156–157
Johnson, Ching: 114–115
Jönsson, Jörgen: 109, 211
Joseph, Curtis "Cujo": 89
Joseph Turner Memorial Cup: 136, 152, 216

Kansas City Scouts: 26
Kazakhstan National Team: 211
Kazakhstan National Women's Team: 214
Kelly Cup: 74
Kenesky, Emil "Pop": 8
Kennedy, Ted: 180–181
Keon, Dave: 118–119, 212
Kerr, Kevin: 58–59, 207
Kewley, Herb: 46, 109, 206, 211
Khabibulin, Nikolai: 60–61, 98, 207
Kharlamov, Valeri: 58–59, 207
Kilrea, Brian: 154, 217
Kim Crouch Collar: 4
King Clancy Memorial Trophy: 172, 219
Kings see Los Angeles Kings
Klagenfurter AC: 83
Knopp, Kevin: 136
Kolesnik, Vitaliy: 109, 211
Koroll, Cliff: 187
Kovalchuk, Ilya: 64, 208
Kroeks, Sari: 108, 211
Kubina, Pavel: 146, 215
Kuznetsov, Evgeny (Genia): 111–112, 115
Kypreos, Nick: 185

Laaksonen, Emma: 108, 211
Labonté, Charline: 60–61, 207
Lady Byng Memorial Trophy: 173, 220 see also Lady Byng Trophy
Lady Byng Trophy: 215
Lafleur, Guy: 39, 41, 118–119, 212, 213
LaFontaine, Pat: 69, 125, 146, 209, 214, 215
Lalonde, Newsy: 180–181
Lamoriello, Lou: 156
Langway, Rod: 147, 215
Lapointe, Guy: 69, 209
Latvian National Team: 207
Laval Mistral: 213
Lecavalier, Vincent: 80, 210
Lee, Anders: 71
Leetch, Brian: 65, 82, 156, 208, 213, 214
Lehtinen, Jere: 85
LeMay, Arthur: 28
Lemieux, Mario: 63, 65, 118–119, 130–131, 208, 212
Leschyshyn, Curtis: 112–113
Lessard, Mario: 213
Lester B. Pearson Award: 219
Lester Patrick Cup: 152, 216
LeSueur, Percy: 39, 60–61, 207
Lethbridge Broncos: 141
Létourneau, Louis: 220
Levins Cup: 74
Lexington Men O' War: 136
Lidstrom, Nicklas: 22, 146, 215
Lightning see Tampa Bay Lightning

Lindbergh, Pelle: 89, 96
Lindsay, Ted: 53, 118–119, 212, 220
Little, Charles: 154, 217
lockout, NHL: 149
"Long Game": 56–57
Lopresti, Pete: 216
Los Angeles Forum: 67
Los Angeles Kings: 10, 66–67, 71, 95, 112, 116, 144–145, 208, 209, 213, 214
Loughlin, Wilf: 48–49
Low, Ron: 89
Luce, Don: 58–59, 207
"lucky loonie": 200
Ludwig, Craig: 79
Lumley, Harry: 126
Lytle, Andy: 100

MacLeish, Rick: 64, 187, 208
Madison Square Garden: 55
Maggs, Darryl: 136–137
Maggs, Dennis: 28
Magnuson, Justin: 52, 206
Mahovlich, Frank: 65, 80, 196–197, 208, 210
Malkin, Evgeni: 80, 210
Manitoban Provincial Team: 206
Maple Leaf Gardens: 25, 52, 53, 72, 116, 179, 206, 220
Maple Leaf Gardens Hockey Magazine: 10
Maples Leafs see Toronto Maple Leafs
Mara, George: 9
Markham Waxers: 2, 4
Marois, Mario: 125, 214
Marsh, Lou: 48–49
Martin, Rick: 64, 208
Marvin, Robin: 120, 212
Masterton, Bill: 219
Mathers, Frank: 140
Maurice Richard Trophy: 172, 219
McCauley, John: 48–49
McDonald, Lanny: 64, 208
McFaul, George: 76
McGill University Redmen: 52, 206
McKenna, Bob: 106
McKenney, Don: 140
McKenzie, Bob: 185
McLelland, Ivan: 47, 206
McNeil, Gerry: 122–123, 208
Mecca, Jack and Peter: 201
Medicine Hat Tigers: 56–57
Meeker, Howie: 180–181, 191
Melgard, Al: 190
Meloche, Gilles: 2, 4
Memorial Cup: 9, 74, 164, 218
Messier, Mark: 41, 121, 213
Messina, Sal: 180–181
Mexican National Team: 211
Michigan-Ontario Hockey League: 216
Mighty Ducks see Anaheim Ducks

Mikita, Stan: 8, 62–63, 114–115
Miller, Gord: 115
Miller, Ryan: 128, 185
Minnesota Blue J's: 212
Minnesota Fighting Saints: 136–137, 208
Minnesota North Stars: 52, 73, 102, 136, 206, 215, 216, 219
Minnesota Whitecaps: 162
Minnesota Wild: 209
"Miracle on Ice": 91, 134
Mississippi Sea Wolves: 74
Modano, Mike: 116–117
Modo: 211
Mogilny, Alexander: 125, 214
Moncton Hawks: 206
Montreal Amateur Athletic Association: 83, 149, 156
Montreal Arena Company: 217
Montreal Axion: 207
Montreal Canadiens: 8, 9, 10, 18, 39, 41, 53, 74, 77, 86, 92, 103, 122–123, 139, 142, 180–181, 187, 205, 208, 209, 212, 213, 219, 220
Montreal Forum: 8, 74
Montreal Herald: 189
Montreal Maroons: 121, 213, 214
Montreal Stars: 162
Montreal Wanderers: 142, 217
Morenz, Howie: 139, 142
Morrison, George: 65, 208
Morrison, Ian "Scotty": 11
Moscow Selects: 27
Mosienko, Bill "Mosie": 54–55
Mott, Morris: 83
Movsessian-Lamoriello, Vicki: 120, 212
Mullen, Joe: 121, 213, 214
Muni, Craig: 112–113, 146, 215
Murphy, Larry: 69, 209
Murphy, Randy: 125, 214
Murray, Glenn: 116–117
Muskegon Fury: 213
Mutual Street Arena: 72
Mylnikov, Sergei: 131

Nashville Knights: 209
Nashville Predators: 210
National Aboriginal Hockey Championships: 206
National Hockey Association (NHA): 150, 180, 220
National Hockey League (NHL): 180
   board of governors: 180
   lockout: 149
   see also All-Star Games, All-Stars, NHL Broadcasters' Association, Stanley Cup and individual teams and awards
National Hockey League Players' Association: 219
National Women's Hockey League: 207, 213

Naylor, Tommy: 79
NCAA: 141, 202, 206, 210, 219
   Division I: 212
   Division II: 212
   Division III: 209
   Frozen Four: 99, 207
Neely, Cam: 20, 106, 107, 116–117, 209
Neilson, Roger: 139
Netherlands National Team: 211
Newell, Dave: 210
New England Fighting Saints: 22
New England Whalers: 136–137
New Jersey Devils: 115, 116, 207, 209, 213, 215, 216
New Mexico Scorpions: 214
News of the World: 185
New York Americans: 100, 115, 142, 213
New York Islanders: 2, 4, 31, 63, 106, 115, 207, 208, 210, 213, 214, 215, 216
New York Rangers: 41, 48–49, 55, 79, 82, 95, 100, 150, 207, 208, 212, 213, 214, 215, 216, 219, 220
NHL see National Hockey League
NHL All-Rookie Team: 215
NHL Broadcasters' Association: 179, 219
NHL Challenge: 56–57
NHL Challenge Cup: 166–167, 192–193
NHL YoungStars Game: 209
Nicholson, Bob: 161
Niedermayer, Rob: 146, 215
Niedermayer, Scott: 68, 114–115, 209, 215
Nieuwendyk, Joe: 146, 215
Niiranen, Eino "Nakki": 204
Nilson, Marcus: 22
Nordli, Ylva Viktoria: 120, 212
Norris, James: 173, 196, 220
Norris Trophy: 82, 215
North York Beatrice Aeros: 213
Norwegian National Women's Team: 212
Nylander, Michael: 58–59, 207

Oates, Adam: 118–119, 212
O'Brien Cup: 149
O'Brien, J.: 150
O'Brien, J. Ambrose: 150
O'Brien Trophy: 150–151
Obydennova, Darya: 214
Ocskay, Gábor: 109, 211
OHA see Ontario Hockey Association
OHL see Ontario Hockey League
Oilers see Edmonton Oilers
Olympia: 213
Olympic Summer Games
   Antwerp, Belgium (1920): 132
   Athens, Greece (1896): 32

Olympic Winter Games: 9, 32–35, 161
   Calgary, Alberta (1988): 132
   Chamonix, France (1924): 158–159
   Garmisch-Partenkirchen, Germany (1936): 5
   Lake Placid, New York (1980): 35, 91, 134, 213
   Lillehammer, Norway (1994): 96
   Nagano, Japan (1998): 192–193, 208, 211, 212, 214
   Oslo, Norway (1952): 185, 188
   Salt Lake City, Utah (2002): 74, 128, 185, 200, 206, 208, 211, 214, 217
   Squaw Valley, California (1960): 43, 134
   St. Moritz, Switzerland (1928): 202
   St. Moritz, Switzerland (1948): 9, 76
   Squaw Valley, California (1960): 43, 134
   Turin, Italy (2006): 56–57, 210, 211, 212
   Vancouver, British Columbia (2010): 39, 74, 128–129, 185, 198, 208
Omsk Avangard: 111–112, 115
Ontario Hockey Association (OHA): 141, 165, 218
Ontario Hockey League (OHL): 165, 218
Ontario Major Junior Hockey League: 141, 217
Ontario Provincial Team: 207
Ontario University Athletics (OUA): 210
Ontario University Athletics Select team: 214
O-Pee-Chee Hockey Star Gum: 16
O'Ree, Willie: 121, 213
O'Reilly, Terry: 68, 209
Original Six: 11, 22, 23
Orr, Bobby: 36–37, 41, 77, 208
Ostberg, Cecilia: 120, 212
Ottawa 67's: 217
Ottawa Civics: 136
Ottawa Cliffsides: 217
Ottawa Junior Canadiens: 9
Ottawa Senators: 6, 207, 213, 215
Ouellette, Caroline: 120, 212
Ovechkin, Alex: 64, 187, 201, 202, 208
Oxford University: 217
Oxford–Cambridge Challenge Shield: 153, 217

Pacific Coast Hockey League (PCHL): 216, 218
Pakarinen, Risto: 198–202, 204
Palmateer, Mike: 102
Pang, Darren: 185
Panthers see Florida Panthers

Parise, Zach: 185
Park, Brad: 58–59, 207
Parkhurst: 18, 19
Parsons, Don: 58–59, 127, 207, 214
Patrick, Lester: 216
Patterson, Bill: 188
pee wee hockey: 77, 112
Penguins see Pittsburgh Penguins
Penney, Steve: 208
Penticton Vees: 47, 206
Pepels, Marion: 108, 211
Peternousek, George: 109, 211
Peters, Jimmy: 55
Philadelphia Flyers: 27, 56–57, 96, 184, 201, 207, 208, 213, 216
Phil Henderson Cup: 216
Phoenix Coyotes: 99, 207
Phoenix Roadrunners: 27, 214
Pimm, Braden: 58–59, 207
Pittsburgh Penguins: 56–57, 71, 72, 74, 91, 112, 116, 156–157, 204, 207, 208, 210, 213, 214, 215
Plante, Jacques: 8, 86–87, 88, 91, 198
Poirier, Steve: 69, 201, 209
Polillo, Paul: 121, 213
Port Huron Border Cats: 213
Port Huron Flags: 136
Potvin, Denis: 106, 121, 213
Predators see Nashville Predators
Presentation Stanley Cup: 174–175
President's Cup: 216
Presidents' Trophy: 173, 220
Preston Rivulettes: 76, 142
Priakin, Sergei: 145
Prince Albert Mintos: 207
Prince George Mohawks: 203
Prince of Wales: 220
Prince of Wales Conference: 220
Prince of Wales Trophy: 150, 173, 204, 220
Pritchard, Phil: 10–11, 198, 200, 201, 202, 203, 204
Professional Hockey Writers' Association: 189, 218, 219, 220
Pronovost, Jean: 64, 208
Providence Reds: 140
Puck, Peter: 187
Pulford, Bob: 53
Purdie, Brad: 109, 211
Puschinig, Sepp: 83

QMJHL see Quebec Major Junior Hockey League
Quad City Mallards: 207, 214
Quebec Bulldogs: 150
Quebec Hockey League: 193, 216
Quebec Major Junior Hockey League (QMJHL): 214, 218
Quebec Nordiques: 27, 63, 112, 115, 145, 209, 213
Quebec Remparts: 214
Queen's Cup: 210
Quinnipiac University: 206
Quinn, Pat: 154, 217

Ralph, Mike: 136
Rangers see New York Rangers
Ranscombe, Hilda: 76, 142
Ratelle, Jean: 58–59, 71, 207
Rayner, Chuck: 212
Rayside-Balfour Sabrecats: 56–57
RBC Cup: 207
Recchi, Mark: 147, 215
Red Army team see Soviet National Team and Russian National Team
Red Wings see Detroit Red Wings
Reid, Maurice H. "Lefty": 11
Renfrew Hockey Club: 180–181
Resch, Glenn "Chico": 2, 4, 60–61, 207
Richard, Henri: 121, 213
Richard, Maurice "Rocket": 20, 63, 65, 118–119, 126–127, 170, 177, 205, 208, 212, 214
Richard, Mike: 127, 214
Richards, Brad: 111, 114–115
Richardson, George: 217
Richter, Mike: 147, 214, 216
Roberts, Gary: 112–113
Roberts, Gordie: 121, 213
Roberts, Juan Pablo: 108, 211
Robertson, Gordie: 185, 188
Robertson, John Ross: 165
Robinson, Larry: 74
Robitaille, Luc: 68, 112–113, 156, 208, 209
Rochester War Memorial Auditorium: 72
Rod, Gilbert: 29
Rollins, Al: 212
Rolston, Brian: 68, 209
Romanian National Team: 214
Ronn, Jyri Petteri: 51
Rookie of the Year: 215, 219
Rooth, Maria: 120, 127, 212, 214
Ross, Art: 180–181, 219
Royal Bank Cup: 56–57
Royal Canadian Air Force Flyers: 9, 76
Royal York Hotel: 196
Roy, Patrick: 92–93
Russian National Junior Team: 56–57, 74, 115
Russian National Team: 21, 25, 26, 44–45, 56–57, 111, 131, 206, 208, 211 see also Soviet National Team
Russian Superleague: 111, 210
Rutherford, Jim: 2, 4
Ryder, Fran: 161
Ryerson University Rams: 206

Sabres see Buffalo Sabres
Saginaw Gears: 136
Sakic, Joe: 20, 68, 114–115, 127, 209, 214
Salei, Ruslan: 214
Salming, Börje: 22
San Diego Mariners: 27

San Jose Sharks: 215
Saskatchewan Provincial Team: 206
Sawchuk, Terry: 60–61, 76, 89, 92, 94–95, 178–179, 207
SC Bern: 211
SC Langnau: 211
Scapinello, Ray "Scampy": 48–49
Schmidt, Milt: 142
Seaman, Daryl K. "Doc": 156–157, 202
Seattle Metropolitans: 216
Second All-Star Team: 85, 209, 210 see also All-Stars, All-Star Games and First All-Star Team
Seiling, Rod: 132
Selänne, Teemu: 85
Selke, Frank J.: 220
Senators see Ottawa Senators
Senior Championship Trophy: 153, 217
Shanahan, Brendan: 121, 213
Sharks see San Jose Sharks
Shaw, Brad: 84
Shawinigan Falls: 193
Shearer, Danny: 141
Sherer, Sue: 132
Shipstads and Johnson Perpetual Challenge Trophy: 171, 218
Shore, Eddie: 104–105
"Showdown": 187
Shutt, Steve: 121, 213
Shyryaev, Valeri: 108, 211
Sinden, Harry: 47, 206
Sittler, Darryl: 118–119, 187, 212
Slap Shot: 136
Slovakian National Team: 214
Small, Sami Jo: 96
Smith, Billy: 147, 216
Smith, Borden: 52, 206
Smith, Brian: 188
Smith, Buddy: 106
Smith, Clint: 210
Smith Falls Seniors (club team): 207
Smith, Gary: 212
Smith, Reginald "Hooley": 121, 213
Smyth, Ryan: 81, 210
Smythe, Conn: 220
Smythe, Stafford: 196
Snell, Wesley: 109, 211
Sorel Black Hawks: 214
South African National Team: 211
Southern Conference (ECHL): 106
Soviet National Team: 45, 71, 91, 106, 132, 134, 166, 206, 207, 212, 213 see also Russian National Junior Team and Russian National Team
Soviet Wings: 27
Spengler, Carl: 169
Spengler Cup: 169
SportsDesk: 184
Sports Network: 184
Staal, Eric: 116–117

Staal, Jordan: 146, 215
Stamkos, Steven: 69, 209
Stanley Cup: 6, 7, 8, 9, 96, 149, 161, 173, 182, 187, 191, 198, 204, 205, 209, 216, 217, 220
1901–02: 83
1902–03: 83
1905–06: 142, 207
1906–07: 142
1907–08: 142, 207
1908–09: 207
1911–12: 150
1912–13: 150
1913–14: 216
1916–17: 216
1924–25: 60–61, 207, 216
1934–35: 213
1935–36: 100
1937–38: 48
1949–50: 217
1950–51: 122–123, 124, 208
1963–64: 213
1969–70: 36–37
1979–80: 216
1980–81: 31, 216
1981–82: 216
1982–83: 216
1983–84: 216
1986–87: 216
1993–94: 82
1994–95: 209
1998–99: 74, 79, 85, 91, 116, 215
1999–2000: 116, 215, 216
2001–02: 213
2002–03: 209, 215
2003–04: 48–49, 98, 209
2005–06: 116, 159, 215
2006–07: 85, 215, 216
2007–08: 56–57, 74, 215
2008–09: 74
2009–10: 56–57, 145, 213
Presentation: 174–175
rings: 156–157
Stanley, Lord of Preston: 149, 161, 175, 194, 217, 220
Stars see Dallas Stars
St. Catharines Tee Pees: 141
Stevens, Scott: 68, 209, 216
Stewart, Bill: 48
Stewart, Nels: 212
Stillman, Cory: 146, 215
St. Louis Blues: 22, 36, 89, 112, 145, 206, 207, 208, 212, 216
St. Louis, Martin: 146, 215
St. Pierre, Kim: 52, 206
Sturm, Marco: 215
Sudbury Cubs: 211
Sudbury Wolves: 46, 139, 206
Sulander, Ari: 60–61, 207
Summer Olympics see Olympic Summer Games
Summit Series, 1972: 45, 71, 106, 118–119, 132, 133, 192–193, 212

Summit Series, 1974: 45, 206
Sushinsky, Maxim: 108, 211
Suter, Ron: 141
Svoboda, Petr: 65, 208
Swedish Elite League: 211
Swedish National Team: 56–57, 96, 198, 207, 211
Swedish National Women's Team: 211, 212, 214
Swiss National Junior Team: 115
Swiss National League: 192–193, 211
Swiss National Team: 56–57
Tampa Bay Lightning: 49, 98, 115, 209, 210, 215
Tapani, Susanna: 201
Tarasov, Anatoly: 9
Taylor, Fred "Cyclone": 6, 121, 177, 180–181, 213
Team Canada see Canadian National Junior Team, Canadian National Team and Canadian National Women's Team
Team Russia see Russian National Junior Team, Russian National Team and Soviet National Team
Team USA see USA National Team and USA National Women's Team
Ted Lindsay Award: 172, 219
Telus Cup: 207
Thibault, Jocelyn: 97, 210, 213
Thornson, Len: 136
Thrashers see Atlanta Thrashers
Time magazine: 201
Toews, Jonathan: 145, 156–157
Toronto Aeros: 212
Toronto Arenas: 72
Toronto Blueshirts: 72
Toronto Maple Leafs: 9, 18, 21, 24, 25, 41, 50–51, 52, 53, 72, 74, 77, 79, 95, 96, 100, 102, 104, 112, 116, 122–123, 124, 126, 138–139, 187, 192–193, 196, 207, 208, 212, 213, 215, 216, 220
Toronto St. Patrick's: 72
Toronto Star: 100
Toronto Toros: 25, 136–137
Torres, Raffi: 140
Towns, Harry: 139
Tradecentre: 187
Trail Smoke Eaters: 132
Tretiak, Vladislav: 133, 212
Trew, Billy: 76
Trottier, Bryan: 31, 81, 210
Trudeau, Pierre Elliot: 9
TSN: 187, 188
Turgeon, Pierre: 146, 215
Turner Cup see Joseph Turner Memorial Cup
Turner, Joe: 216

Udvari, Frank: 81, 210
UHL see United Hockey League
Ullman, Norm: 112–113, 193
Unger, Gary: 22
Union College: 52, 206
United Hockey League (UHL): 207, 213
United States Hockey League: 71
University of Alberta Pandas: 212
University of Michigan Wolverines: 141
University of Minnesota-Duluth Bulldogs: 212
University of Western Ontario Mustangs: 97, 210
University of Wisconsin Badgers: 99, 210
Upper Deck NHL All-Rookie Team Trophy: 171, 218
USA National Team: 43, 56–57, 91, 128, 134–135, 166, 213, 214, 219
USA National Women's Team: 56–57, 208, 211, 212

Vaasan Sport: 211
Vachon, Rogie: 10, 103
Vaive, Rick: 64, 208
Valadas, Jack: 108, 211
Vancouver Blazers: 208
Vancouver Canucks: 26, 56–57, 66, 139, 208, 215
Vancouver Giants: 56–57
Vancouver Millionaires: 6
Van Horne, Jim: 184
Verbeek, Pat: 74
Verdun Junior Canadiens: 214
Vernon Vipers: 207
Vetter, Jessie: 99
Vezina, Georges: 219
Vezina Trophy: 89, 92, 173, 216, 219, 220
Victoria Cougars: 207, 216
Voima hockey club: 198, 199, 204
Vokoun, Tomas: 147, 216

Wales Conference: 220
Walton, Mike: 22
Warhol, Andy: 29
Washington Capitals: 71, 89, 106, 115, 202, 207, 208, 213, 215, 216
Watson, Bugsy: 21
Watson, Sandy: 9
Wembley Lions: 217
Wendell, Krissy: 120, 212
West Division: 219
Western Canadian Hockey League: 210
Western Canadian Junior Hockey League (WCJHL): 141
Western Conference: 219
Western Hockey League (WHL): 56–57, 141, 192–193, 216, 218

Western Professional Hockey League: 76, 214
Western Women's Hockey League: 162
WHA see World Hockey Association
Whalers see Hartford Whalers
Whitby Dunlops: 44–45, 47, 206
Wichita Thunder: 208
Wickenheiser, Doug: 79
Wickenheiser, Hayley: 73, 77, 120, 212
Wieland, Markus: 108, 211
William M. Jennings Trophy: 172, 219
Williamson, Brad: 79
Wilson, Stacey: 120, 212
Winberg, Pernilla: 120, 212
Windsor Hotel: 180–181
Winnipeg Falcons: 132
Winnipeg Jets: 102, 215
Winnipeg Monarchs: 47, 206
Winnipeg Victorias: 182
Winston Churchill Cup: 217
Winter Olympics see Olympic Winter Games
Women's World Championships: 56–57, 96, 132, 211, 212, 214, 217
World Championships: 9, 56–57, 132, 139, 158–159, 206, 207, 210, 211, 214, 217
World Cup: 166–167, 192–193, 216
World Hockey Association (WHA): 22, 45, 48–49, 74, 83, 91, 136–137, 206, 208, 215, 216
World Junior Championships: 56–57, 74, 115, 168, 210
World Senior Championship Trophy: 149
World Under-17 Championships: 207
World Under-18 Championships: 207
World Wide Gum: 16
Worsley, Gump: 147, 212, 216
Worters, Roy: 28, 100
WPHL see Western Professional Hockey League
Wregget, Ken: 77

Yakushev, Alexander: 106
Yzerman, Steve: 112, 116–117, 146, 156, 215

Zaugg, Jinelle: 81, 210